Aloha!

The 2,000-Word Guide To Writing

How to Write Quick, Clever, Concise, Clear, Copacetic, Artistic, Professional, Sophisticated, and Gorgeous Prose

Jefferson Rose

Alderhanna Publishing

ISBN 978-1-943177-94-3

Contents

The 2,000-Word Guide to Writing

Writing well is romance between pen and paper. Or love with a laptop. Either way, this Lothario needs a toolbox. A writer's toolbox is a beautiful thing, and its queen is motif. This correspondent thinks motif to be a future, a future where there might be no plot, perhaps no characters, yet oodles of motif. We'll talk motif plenty. And we'll quickly fly through the whole scribe shebang.

A personal writing toolbox harbors a store of strong verbs, specific nouns, juicy adjectives, few adverbs, uncommon common words, and often the use of synonyms rather than the exact word choice as synonyms create surprise. Using the wrong word in a sentence that still makes it right creates surprise. Writing in metaphor within a sentence also provides surprise. Writing all three acts in a single sentence of arc creates surprise.

Writing once involved lots of coffee to get chatty followed by hours of chopping the copy. That's ancient history, now we have guidelines to use.

About writing, we say there are guidelines, yet no rules. And there are thoughts. Unity is achievable. A story or essay should be about one thing and every sentence should speak to that one thing. Except, this author pens stories about five or eight or sixteen elements. Can many elements blend together into unity? Perhaps yes? Maybe not? Our very literate neighbor thinks no. He says one can't tell what the hell statement is being made with a whole circus on the page. Our answer, writing is pissing off one's neighbor. Writing also is rhythm; surprise; removing words every editing pass; creating paragraphs at times that are in 3-act structure; encapsulating thoughts in crisp, daring, well-described, and unusual ways; perhaps having a central metaphor for a work; perhaps strewing throughout metaphor, simile and comparison.

This correspondent arrived into the world in a house full of books and quickly he knew he would write one of his own. In high school, he turned in the first book report he had written in his schooling. He received a grade of "F" for his effort, the lowest grade possible. The note written by the teacher on his report read, "How can you turn in a report on a book you haven't read?" He had read the book, he could not think nor write. (Just to let you know, the book was Catch-22.) It was going to be a long road for him and today he is a ways down that road. Rather than describe the path he has walked, let him tell of the signposts he has seen on his journey.

Idea. Ideas are everywhere, use a big one. Or use a little one. Write subtly. Or write in headlines. Can't find an idea? Crack open a book. Eavesdrop at the coffee shop. Flip on the television. Think back in time. Have six cups of coffee and blather till something comes out.

Stories and essays. The title and first sentence should kill. And often, when a title or first sentence comes to one, the story writes itself.

The Routine Rule. "Show don't tell." Bullshit. Showing and telling are both tools in the writer's box. When confused, show, then tell. Often here, one is talking about showing gesture or expression, not writing a million-page book that shows absolutely everything. Also, it's not saying, "A cliff sat behind the beach." Show the cliff, show the beach. "A tall cliff of crumbling chalk in yellows, browns, and blacks sifted down to meet the white sand beach, the waves of high tide churning these colors into a modern-art painting." Be visual.

Metaphors, similes, and comparisons. Create a central metaphor for your work. Or not. If so, say you're writing about office politics. Use water. Lakes are the resources. Rivers and streams connect all to the data, to the gossip, and to each office staff. Oceans of uncertainty, pools of knowledge, and rivulets of thought. Cloudbursts of idea, floods of paperwork, sprinkles of bonhomie, and whirlpools of office romance. Use metaphor and comparison and simile all day if you want to. If you're writing pulp, snappy similes are a must. "His memos get passed faster than bad chutney at the bus station."

Character. Characters and character arcs (the change in a character during a story) can be book-long or wrapped up in a few words. Use some flair when describing a character:

Elliot took measured strides down the city sidewalks from the hotel, not the long strides of his youth. His look, black cowboy hat and boots, spoke of his country honk. Tan sports jacket, jeans, and white cotton shirt with little printed cacti completed the ensemble. When in Rome, do as you do at home. Shaggy-coiffed Elliot is a man whose expression was that of a spark. His eyes spoke to all with a mischievous twinkle as he walked through low-rise districts distinctively different from the skyscraper canyons of Wall Street and Midtown.

Even a waitress appearing at dinner without a speaking part can reflect something important in the story by using a few words to describe the character and her arc. This could be called a John Prine arc—in one song, Prine nailed an arc in eleven words,

"She was a level-headed woman on the road to alcohol."

Verbs. Use strong verbs. In a first draft, one might write. "She was in West Palm Beach." In the second draft, you'll write, "Ensconced in a West Palm condo, she partied with sand and sun tans."

Nouns. Strong nouns are necessary and being specific with them is the way to go. It's not a restaurant, it's a diner. It's not a diner, it's a greasy spoon, it's not a greasy spoon, it's Mort's Disappoint Joint. It's not a flood, it's an inundation. It's not an inundation, it's a deluge. It's not a deluge, it's a tsunami. It's not a tsunami, it's Noah's Flood.

Adverbs. "Don't use adverbs." Bullshit. I think the intent is say, use exact and strong verbs. If there's no verb that fits, add the adverb (usually preceding the verb.)

Adjectives. "Don't use adjectives." Bullshit. Adjectives should be selected from the juice section of the grocery as there is nothing better than a juicy adjective.

Concision. Removing words from a draft is a talent to be acquired. Have fun with surgery. Take a draft of yours, put down the pen, pick up the penknife. Go to town. Narrative, dialogue, everything.

Word choice and sentences. Continually search for juicy adjectives, synonyms, uncommon yet common words, places in which to use a word wrong that still makes a sentence right. Invert sentences the way a musician inverts musical lines. This is done by starting with a different word. Pick a word from the middle or the end of the sentence—an object, conjunction, participle, verb, or whatever. Also, use parallel structure in sentences here and there, as well as parallel logic.

Here's a boring first sentence:

"The donut shop sat by the military academy that was upstream from the capital."

Here's a fancy-pants first sentence with strong nouns, strong verbs, parallel structure, and adjective "copacetic" used in an unusual or perhaps verb-like way:

"The Donut Shoppe, a white-washed relic adjacent to and copacetic with the United States

Naval Academy, bathed in a mist of Chesapeake chop same as it bathed in a fog of national politics."

Variety. Vary your sentences, start with an article, a verb, a noun, a participle, a gerund, mix it up. Consider length of sentences and mix that up, too. Changing rhythms. The first word of a sentence is a position of strength. Same with the final word of a sentence. The final sentence of a paragraph is where the emphasis naturally falls. Exploit this.

Rhythm. Use short sentences in the mix. Or shorter. Combine straight-ahead sentences with some containing several phrases or clauses.

Foreshadowing. A hint to what will happen. Be direct, or subtle, or prophetic. Perhaps to use symbols. Or give a hint that leads the reader astray on a red herring (Often used in mysteries.)

In Romeo and Juliet, the balcony scene, Romeo suggests death at the hands of the guards would be better than a life without Juliet. We glimpse the future.

In Tolkien's work, as a passel of characters enters the forest, the author strongly foreshadowed as much as anyone ever has in literature when he wrote in all capital letters, "STAY ON THE PATH."

Chekov foreshadowed in his famous scene by having a pistol sitting on a coffee table. The way Chekov put it was, "If you see a gun in the second act, it must go off in the third."

Surprise. Surprise is the best. Surprise by using a synonym, not the exact word. Surprise by creating a sentence using metaphor, not reality. Surprise by using uncommon common words. Surprise by using the wrong word in a sentence that still comes out right. And story surprise. Here's a sample about a hitchhiker and a pair who pull over to pick him up.

In Biloxi, it came down in buckets. The interstate, a car wash. Lolita and Jack, blinded. They pulled under an over-through and parked next to several other flashers-on vehicles and a glum-looking hitchhiker. Lolita dialed down the window, said, "Hop in!" He slid into the back seat.

Jack leaned over the seat and said to the damp and now smiling gentleman, "Lolita and Jack, we're on our way to California."

"No you're not," he said.

"We're looking for the future of America," Jack said.

"I've read Kerouac and I'm familiar with Lolita and you guys are fine, but you're headed east, not west." He leaned over the front seat and pointed to a road sign reading, 'Tallahassee 303.'

Rainwater blurring the windshield view had confused the duo's directions in the storm. "We'll take you where you're going, then flip around."

Theft. There's some hammer that says, "Bad artists borrow, good artists steal." This correspondent guesses one must make those choices and most acknowledge the theft. Here's a quote by Jean-Jacques Rousseau, updated to 2020.

> "Man was born free,
> and everywhere he is in society."

Weirdness. Here's a present tense sentence amid a past tense passage. Why? I don't know, the whole story is weird. Weird past tense, then out of the blue comes a present-tense thought. The thought could be described as Fourth Person Point-of-View – disembodied.

Asleep one morning while half-awake and conscious in a way, Chatterley saw where his life made sense, although it made sense in a manner one would not expect. Fluorescent lighting had always unsettled him. Yet, fluorescence had provided hints about when stressful moments in life occurred, and stressful moments tended to occur where fluorescent lighting was involved. Even the glow of a television tube creates havoc, you know. Chatterley had posed questions to himself before he slumbered. On that morning, his subconscious thrust the answers into his consciousness. He had used the trick of the creatives and found peace.

Dialogue. Listen to people speak. To link the thoughts of two people in discussion, perhaps restate a bit of the prior dialogue as part of the response. Perhaps the opposite--go off-the-nose plenty as people tend to not respond directly. "Do you want to go to the cinema?" he said. "Popcorn makes me puke," she said.

Motif. Motif will be queen in the future. As a series of reflections on the theme, or as an artistic accompaniment to the composition, either accomplished in a repeated manner, motif is both glue and advertisement. Create motifs that reflect a central point or perhaps a juxtaposition of a central point. Or not. Or both. Motif as a subtheme can be a logical reflection of a story line or just some artsy added decor. Motif can be confused with a central metaphor. Using a motif of water and using a central metaphor of water can be the same thing, sort of.

Genius scribe Tom Robbins is the man that introduced motif to this author.

Motif can be confused with theme and symbol. What's to remember is theme is an abstract element while motifs are constructed with concrete elements. Symbols appear once, motifs repeat. Can a writer author a piece where motif is abstract? Why not. Can repeated symbols be symbolism and not motif? Well, here the two different things might be the same thing.

Here's Hemingway doing motif:

The motif contained in 'Old Man and the Sea' has crucifixion imagery. The main character, Santiago, is far out to sea in a small boat with a big fish on the hook. He cut the palms of his hand with his fishing line, this leads readers to think about the stigmata of Christ on the Cross. When attacked by sharks, Santiago utters sounds a man would make if he were "having nails driven though his hands."

Theme. Is what the work is about. World peace, great loss, businessmen learning the sense of community of Native peoples.

Symbolism: Let's say a stranger arrives in town. That's the oldest trope in the world. If the town is inhabited by demons from Hell, and the first thing the main character sees upon entering town is a red light. Well, there you have it. Symbolism and foreshadowing.

Tropes. Tropes are anything you can get away with.

Overused Words. "Was, but, the, then, and that." These are words to watch out for as they oft can be repeated. Repeated words can stand out in the wrong way. Or sometimes repetition is a dream, a strength, a poetry. Anyway, use a search function to locate and fix occurrences of overused words.

"That" can be superfluous at times:

"Kip reminded Cecelia that lit class came next and the writing assignment was due."

"Kip reminded Cecelia lit class came next and the writing assignment was due. "

Was and But and The

 "He was attracted to art but was confused about the many styles."

"Attracted to art, its many styles confused him."

The above sentence loses the "was," "but," and "the."

On "was," vary sentences by using strong verbs.

On "but," synonyms for the word "but" include although, however, nevertheless, on the other hand, still, though, yet, besides, and more. The word "but" oft is overused and oft there is a synonym with a meaning more in line with what the sentence is saying. The word "but" implies some opposition to the foregoing words, yet oft the word choice to be used should not declare opposition, rather it should supply a meaning of "in addition" or "in juxtaposition" or similar.

On "the," synonyms are "a" and "an" and similar to but, using a greater variety of sentence structures might reduce the number. Try inverting sentences. Just start with a verb, an object, a participle, a conjunction, whatever to get the sentences varied. Often a slight restructuring, use of a pronoun or possessive pronoun, or substitution with a noun or proper noun loses the "the." Also, "The The" is a fab musical group from the eighties.

On "then," this word often can simply go away.

Prepositions. "Don't end a sentence with a preposition." Bullshit. I don't know where that rule came from. But there's a great joke about it.

A Texan arrived for his first day at Harvard

University and found himself lost in the yard. He stopped a professor who was walking by and said to him, "Howdy Pardner, could y'all tell me where that there library is at?"

The professor couldn't believe his ears. "What did you say?" he said.

The Texan again said, "Howdy pardner, could y'all tell me where that there library is at?"

The professor became indignant, "You can't talk like that at Harvard University. I mean, you've ended your sentence with a preposition. Try to do better!"

The Texan shuffled for a second and said, "Well pardner, could y'all tell me where that there library is at... ... ...asshole!"

Point-of-View. Use this handy POV Cheat Sheet to structure the voice.

First Person—Good for close psychological distance, like when you want to instantly immerse the reader in the world of the main character. When the main character pukes, so do you. "I call that diner the disappoint joint. It makes me puke."

First Person—Omniscient—Good for when your main character is a clairvoyant. This character knows whenever anyone pukes. "I know somebody is puking at the diner right now. His name is Benny Molto and he had the Number Six."

Second Person—Singular—Good for when you want the reader to puke. "You are in the diner puking your guts out."

Second Person—Plural—Good for when you want the reader to know all of the readers are puking. "We are in the diner watching people step out back and puke."

Third Person—Limited—This is for when you don't want the main character to know someone is puking but you want the reader to know someone somewhere is puking. "He knew not that many patrons were out back puking."

Third Person Multiple—This is for when all characters puke by themselves. "Benny felt like puking, across the city, Maynard was behind the diner. He, too, was puking."

Third Person—Omniscient—Good for when everyone's puking needs description. "Benny felt like puking, across the city, Maynard was puking behind the diner. Everyone in Mexico City was, at that moment, puking."

Fourth Person—Omniscient—Good for when God needs to describe everyone puking. 'A voice came from the sky, "Thou shalt puke!" And all of the peoples of the Earth puked.'

Fourth Person—Disembodied—Good for when a character from beyond the grave describes characters puking. 'A voice from the past said, "Mildred, your cooking always made me puke."'

Fourth Person—Limited—Good for when God is not allowed to see that the American citizen looks at his politicians and pukes. "Go forth and multiply," said the lord. Yet it was the politicians who multiplied and they made all of the citizens puke.

Do know, some of the selections above do not officially exist.

Creativity. A clever trick exists among creatives. At night before they slumber, they pose questions to themselves. How will the writer get the fiends to expose themselves? How will the artist paint onto a canvas what is inside his mind? The poet asks what word rhymes with newfangled yet means timeless? Some folk sleep on a problem. A creative takes this further by instructing his subconscious with questions to solve the problem. Overnight.

Here are the results:

One morning, the writer realized the fiends would think themselves invisible, after all, they had coated each other with the lemon juice that creates invisible messages on paper? We cannot be seen, now we can rob banks! For the writer, this was the answer.

The artist awoke with the thought that he himself should be painted as crazily spinning in the center of the canvas against a background of an insanely-painted city scene. This, the inability to adapt to everyday life!

The poet had a dream. The newfangled of today mattered none as time always found a way to become untangled!

That's that. Now put on a pot of coffee, get out the pen. And get out the penknife.

Cover. The image on the front cover of the book are notes written by H. R. Haldeman to record the treason Richard Nixon entered into by secretly treating with South Vietnam when Nixon was a candidate for the Presidency. His conniving was successful, no peace treaty would be signed that would win the election for Nixon's opponent. Nixon exposed soldiers to years more of war for his political victory. The former president killed his own troops.

—60—

Before we hit the classic literature placed at the end of this tome, let's look at some rules created by many writers chipping in over the years with lovely, sarcastic thoughts that teach one way more about writing than this correspondent ever could:

1. About those sentence fragments.
2. Always pick on the correct idiom.
3. Also, avoid awkward or affected alliteration.
4. Analogies in writing are like feathers on a snake.
5. And don't start a sentence with a conjunction.
6. Avoid alliteration. Always.
7. Avoid trendy locutions that sound flaky.
8. Avoid cliches like the plague. They're old hat.
9. A writer must not shift your point of view.
10. Be more or less specific.
11. Comparisons are as bad as clichés.
12. Contractions aren't necessary.
13. Corect spelling is esential.
14. Do not put statements in the negative form.
15. Don't be redundant and don't use more words than necessary or be highly superfluous.
16. Don't overuse exclamation marks!!
17. Don't use commas, which aren't necessary.
18. Don't use no double negatives.
19. Don't write run-on sentences, they are hard to read.
20. Eliminate quotations. As Ralph Waldo Emerson said, "I hate quotations. Tell me what you know."
21. Employ the vernacular.
22. Eschew ampersands & abbreviations, etc.
23. Even if a mixed metaphor sings, it should be derailed.
24. Everyone should be careful to use a singular pronoun with singular nouns in their writing.
25. Exaggeration is a billion times worse than understatement.

26. Foreign words and phrases are not apropos.

27. Go around the barn at high noon to avoid colloquialisms.

28. If any word is improper at the end of a sentence, a linking verb is.

29. If you reread your work, you can find on rereading that a great deal of repetition can be avoided by rereading and editing.

30. Its important to use your apostrophe's correctly.

31. Just between you and I, case is important.

32. Never, ever use repetitive redundancies.

33. Never use a long word when a diminutive one will do.

34. One should never generalize.

35. One-word sentences? Eliminate.

36. Parenthetical remarks (however relevant) are unnecessary.

37. Place pronouns as close as possible, especially in long sentences, as of ten or more words, to their antecedents.

38. Prepositions are terrible words to end sentences with.

39. Proofread your writing to see if any words out and to avoid misteaks.

40. Remember to never split an infinitive.

41. Take the bull by the hand, and avoid mixing metaphors.

42. The adverb always follows the verb.

43. The passive voice is to be avoided.

44. Understatement is absolutely, positively best.

45. Unqualified superlatives are the worst of all.

46. Verbs has to agree with their subject.

47. Who needs rhetorical questions?

48. Writing carefully, dangling participles must be avoided.

49. Last, but not least, avoid cliche's like the plague. (They're old hat.)

The Raven

Edgar Allan Poe

Once upon a midnight dreary, while I pondered, weak and
weary,
Over many a quaint and curious volume of forgotten lore—
While I nodded, nearly napping, suddenly there came a
tapping,
As of some one gently rapping, rapping at my chamber door.
"'Tis some visitor," I muttered, "tapping at my chamber
door—
Only this and nothing more."
Ah, distinctly I remember it was in the bleak December;
And each separate dying ember wrought its ghost upon the
floor.
Eagerly I wished the morrow;—vainly I had sought to borrow
From my books surcease of sorrow—sorrow for the lost
Lenore—
For the rare and radiant maiden whom the angels name
Lenore—
Nameless here for evermore.
And the silken, sad, uncertain rustling of each purple curtain
Thrilled me—filled me with fantastic terrors never felt before;
So that now, to still the beating of my heart, I stood repeating
"'Tis some visitor entreating entrance at my chamber door—
Some late visitor entreating entrance at my chamber door;—
This it is and nothing more."
Presently my soul grew stronger; hesitating then no longer,
"Sir," said I, "or Madam, truly your forgiveness I implore;

But the fact is I was napping, and so gently you came rapping,
And so faintly you came tapping, tapping at my chamber door,
That I scarce was sure I heard you"—here I opened wide the door;—
Darkness there and nothing more.
Deep into that darkness peering, long I stood there wondering, fearing,
Doubting, dreaming dreams no mortal ever dared to dream before;
But the silence was unbroken, and the stillness gave no token,
And the only word there spoken was the whispered word, "Lenore?"
This I whispered, and an echo murmured back the word, "Lenore!"—
Merely this and nothing more.
Back into the chamber turning, all my soul within me burning,
Soon again I heard a tapping somewhat louder than before.
"Surely," said I, "surely that is something at my window lattice;
Let me see, then, what thereat is, and this mystery explore—
Let my heart be still a moment and this mystery explore;—
'Tis the wind and nothing more!"
Open here I flung the shutter, when, with many a flirt and flutter,
In there stepped a stately Raven of the saintly days of yore;
Not the least obeisance made he; not a minute stopped or stayed he;
But, with mien of lord or lady, perched above my chamber door—
Perched upon a bust of Pallas just above my chamber door—
Perched, and sat, and nothing more.
Then this ebony bird beguiling my sad fancy into smiling,
By the grave and stern decorum of the countenance it wore,

"Though thy crest be shorn and shaven, thou," I said, "art sure no craven,
Ghastly grim and ancient Raven wandering from the Nightly shore—
Tell me what thy lordly name is on the Night's Plutonian shore!"
Quoth the Raven "Nevermore."
Much I marvelled this ungainly fowl to hear discourse so plainly,
Though its answer little meaning—little relevancy bore;
For we cannot help agreeing that no living human being
Ever yet was blessed with seeing bird above his chamber door—
Bird or beast upon the sculptured bust above his chamber door,
With such name as "Nevermore."
But the Raven, sitting lonely on the placid bust, spoke only
That one word, as if his soul in that one word he did outpour.
Nothing farther then he uttered—not a feather then he fluttered—
Till I scarcely more than muttered "Other friends have flown before—
On the morrow he will leave me, as my Hopes have flown before."
Then the bird said "Nevermore."
Startled at the stillness broken by reply so aptly spoken,
"Doubtless," said I, "what it utters is its only stock and store
Caught from some unhappy master whom unmerciful Disaster
Followed fast and followed faster till his songs one burden bore—
Till the dirges of his Hope that melancholy burden bore
Of 'Never—nevermore'."
But the Raven still beguiling all my fancy into smiling,

Straight I wheeled a cushioned seat in front of bird, and bust and door;
Then, upon the velvet sinking, I betook myself to linking
Fancy unto fancy, thinking what this ominous bird of yore—
What this grim, ungainly, ghastly, gaunt, and ominous bird of yore
Meant in croaking "Nevermore."

This I sat engaged in guessing, but no syllable expressing
To the fowl whose fiery eyes now burned into my bosom's core;
This and more I sat divining, with my head at ease reclining
On the cushion's velvet lining that the lamp-light gloated o'er,
But whose velvet-violet lining with the lamp-light gloating o'er,
Sheshall press, ah, nevermore!

Then, methought, the air grew denser, perfumed from an unseen censer
Swung by Seraphim whose foot-falls tinkled on the tufted floor.
"Wretch," I cried, "thy God hath lent thee—by these angels he hath sent thee
Respite—respite and nepenthe from thy memories of Lenore;
Quaff, oh quaff this kind nepenthe and forget this lost Lenore!"
Quoth the Raven "Nevermore."

"Prophet!" said I, "thing of evil!—prophet still, if bird or devil!—
Whether Tempter sent, or whether tempest tossed thee here ashore,
Desolate yet all undaunted, on this desert land enchanted—
On this home by Horror haunted—tell me truly, I implore—
Is there—is there balm in Gilead?—tell me—tell me, I implore!"
Quoth the Raven "Nevermore."

"Prophet!" said I, "thing of evil!—prophet still, if bird or
devil!
By that Heaven that bends above us—by that God we both
adore—
Tell this soul with sorrow laden if, within the distant Aidenn,
It shall clasp a sainted maiden whom the angels name
Lenore—
Clasp a rare and radiant maiden whom the angels name
Lenore."
Quoth the Raven "Nevermore."

"Be that word our sign of parting, bird or fiend!" I shrieked,
upstarting—
"Get thee back into the tempest and the Night's Plutonian
shore!
Leave no black plume as a token of that lie thy soul hath
spoken!
Leave my loneliness unbroken!—quit the bust above my door!
Take thy beak from out my heart, and take thy form from off
my door!"
Quoth the Raven "Nevermore."

And the Raven, never flitting, still is sitting, still is sitting
On the pallid bust of Pallas just above my chamber door;
And his eyes have all the seeming of a demon's that is
dreaming,
And the lamp-light o'er him streaming throws his shadow on
the floor;
And my soul from out that shadow that lies floating on the
floor
Shall be lifted—nevermore!
fin

Araby

James Joyce

NORTH RICHMOND STREET being blind, was a quiet street except at the hour when the Christian Brothers' School set the boys free. An uninhabited house of two storeys stood at the blind end, detached from its neighbours in a square ground The other houses of the street, conscious of decent lives within them, gazed at one another with brown imperturbable faces.

The former tenant of our house, a priest, had died in the back drawing-room. Air, musty from having been long enclosed, hung in all the rooms, and the waste room behind the kitchen was littered with old useless papers. Among these I found a few paper-covered books, the pages of which were curled and damp: *The Abbot*, by Walter Scott, *The Devout Communnicant* and *The Memoirs of Vidocq*. I liked the last best because its leaves were yellow. The wild garden behind the house contained a central apple-tree and a few straggling bushes under one of which I found the late tenant's rusty bicycle-pump. He had been a very charitable priest; in his will he had left all his money to institutions and the furniture of his house to his sister.

When the short days of winter came dusk fell before we had well eaten our dinners. When we met in the street the houses had grown sombre. The space of sky above us was the colour of ever-changing violet and towards it the lamps of the street lifted their feeble lanterns. The cold air stung us and we played till our bodies glowed. Our shouts echoed in the silent street. The career of our play brought us through the dark muddy lanes behind the houses where we ran the gauntlet of the rough tribes from the cottages, to the back doors of the dark dripping gardens where odours arose from the ashpits, to the dark odorous stables where a coachman smoothed and combed the horse or shook music from the buckled harness. When we returned to the street light from the kitchen windows had filled the areas. If my uncle was seen turning the corner we hid in the shadow until we had seen him safely housed. Or if Mangan's sister came out on the doorstep to call her brother in to his tea we watched her from our shadow peer up and down the street. We waited to see whether she would remain or go in and, if she remained, we left our shadow and walked up to Mangan's steps resignedly. She was waiting for us, her figure defined by the light from the half-opened door. Her brother always teased her before he obeyed and I stood by the railings looking at her. Her dress swung as she moved her body and the soft rope of her hair tossed from side to side.

Every morning I lay on the floor in the front parlour watching her door. The blind was pulled down to within an inch of the sash so that I could not be seen. When she came out on the doorstep my heart leaped. I ran to the hall, seized my books and followed her. I kept her brown figure always in my eye and, when we came near the point at which our ways diverged, I quickened my pace and passed her. This happened morning after morning. I had never spoken to her, except for a few casual words, and yet her name was like a summons to all my foolish blood.

Her image accompanied me even in places the most hostile to romance. On Saturday evenings when my aunt went marketing I had to go to carry some of the parcels. We walked through the flaring streets, jostled by drunken men and bargaining women, amid the curses of labourers, the shrill litanies of shop-boys who stood on guard by the barrels of pigs' cheeks, the nasal chanting of street-singers, who sang a come-all-you about O'Donovan Rossa, or a ballad about the troubles in our native land. These noises converged in a single sensation of life for me: I imagined that I bore my chalice safely through a throng of foes. Her name sprang to my lips at moments in strange prayers and praises which I myself did not understand. My eyes were often full of tears (I could not tell why) and at times a flood from my heart seemed to pour itself out into my bosom. I thought little of the future. I did not know whether I would ever speak to her or not or, if I spoke to her, how I could tell her of my confused adoration. But my body was like a harp and her words and gestures were like fingers running upon the wires.

One evening I went into the back drawing-room in which the priest had died. It was a dark rainy evening and there was no sound in the house. Through one of the broken panes I heard the rain impinge upon the earth, the fine incessant needles of water playing in the sodden beds. Some distant lamp or lighted window gleamed below me. I was thankful that I could see so little. All my senses seemed to desire to veil themselves and, feeling that I was about to slip from them, I pressed the palms of my hands together until they trembled, murmuring: "O love! O love!" many times.

At last she spoke to me. When she addressed the first words to me I was so confused that I did not know what to answer. She asked me was I going to Araby. I forgot whether I answered yes or no. It would be a splendid bazaar, she said she would love to go.

"And why can't you?" I asked.

While she spoke she turned a silver bracelet round and round her wrist. She could not go, she said, because there would be a retreat that week in her convent. Her brother and two other boys were fighting for their caps and I was alone at the railings. She held one of the spikes, bowing her head towards me. The light from the lamp opposite our door caught the white curve of her neck, lit up her hair that rested there and, falling, lit up the hand upon the railing. It fell over one side of her dress and caught the white border of a petticoat, just visible as she stood at ease.

"It's well for you," she said.

"If I go," I said, "I will bring you something."

What innumerable follies laid waste my waking and sleeping thoughts after that evening! I wished to annihilate the tedious intervening days. I chafed against the work of school. At night in my bedroom and by day in the classroom her image came between me and the page I strove to read. The syllables of the word Araby were called to me through the silence in which my soul luxuriated and cast an Eastern enchantment over me. I asked for leave to go to the bazaar on Saturday night. My aunt was surprised and hoped it was not some Freemason affair. I answered few questions in class. I watched my master's face pass from amiability to sternness; he hoped I was not beginning to idle. I could not call my wandering thoughts together. I had hardly any patience with the serious work of life which, now that it stood between me and my desire, seemed to me child's play, ugly monotonous child's play.

On Saturday morning I reminded my uncle that I wished to go to the bazaar in the evening. He was fussing at the hallstand, looking for the hat-brush, and answered me curtly:

"Yes, boy, I know."

As he was in the hall I could not go into the front parlour and lie at the window. I left the house in bad humour and walked slowly towards the school. The air was pitilessly raw and already my heart misgave me.

When I came home to dinner my uncle had not yet been home. Still it was early. I sat staring at the clock for some time and. when its ticking began to irritate me, I left the room. I mounted the staircase and gained the upper part of the house. The high cold empty gloomy rooms liberated me and I went from room to room singing. From the front window I saw my companions playing below in the street. Their cries reached me weakened and indistinct and, leaning my forehead against the cool glass, I looked over at the dark house where she lived. I may have stood there for an hour, seeing nothing but the brown-clad figure cast by my imagination, touched discreetly by the lamplight at the curved neck, at the hand upon the railings and at the border below the dress.

When I came downstairs again I found Mrs. Mercer sitting at the fire. She was an old garrulous woman, a pawnbroker's widow, who collected used stamps for some pious purpose. I had to endure the gossip of the tea-table. The meal was prolonged beyond an hour and still my uncle did not come. Mrs. Mercer stood up to go: she was sorry she couldn't wait any longer, but it was after eight o'clock and she did not like to be out late as the night air was bad for her. When she had gone I began to walk up and down the room, clenching my fists. My aunt said:

"I'm afraid you may put off your bazaar for this night of Our Lord."

At nine o'clock I heard my uncle's latchkey in the halldoor. I heard him talking to himself and heard the hallstand rocking when it had received the weight of his overcoat. I could interpret these signs. When he was midway through his dinner I asked him to give me the money to go to the bazaar. He had forgotten.

"The people are in bed and after their first sleep now," he said.

I did not smile. My aunt said to him energetically:

"Can't you give him the money and let him go?
You've kept him late enough as it is."

My uncle said he was very sorry he had forgotten. He
said he believed in the old saying: "All work and no
play makes Jack a dull boy." He asked me where I
was going and, when I had told him a second time he
asked me did I know The Arab's Farewell to his
Steed. When I left the kitchen he was about to recite
the opening lines of the piece to my aunt.

I held a florin tightly in my hand as I strode down
Buckingham Street towards the station. The sight of
the streets thronged with buyers and glaring with gas
recalled to me the purpose of my journey. I took my
seat in a third-class carriage of a deserted train. After
an intolerable delay the train moved out of the station
slowly. It crept onward among ruinous house and
over the twinkling river. At Westland Row Station a
crowd of people pressed to the carriage doors; but the
porters moved them back, saying that it was a special
train for the bazaar. I remained alone in the bare
carriage. In a few minutes the train drew up beside an
improvised wooden platform. I passed out on to the
road and saw by the lighted dial of a clock that it was
ten minutes to ten. In front of me was a large building
which displayed the magical name.

I could not find any sixpenny entrance and, fearing that the bazaar would be closed, I passed in quickly through a turnstile, handing a shilling to a weary-looking man. I found myself in a big hall girdled at half its height by a gallery. Nearly all the stalls were closed and the greater part of the hall was in darkness. I recognised a silence like that which pervades a church after a service. I walked into the centre of the bazaar timidly. A few people were gathered about the stalls which were still open. Before a curtain, over which the words Cafe Chantant were written in coloured lamps, two men were counting money on a salver. I listened to the fall of the coins.

Remembering with difficulty why I had come I went over to one of the stalls and examined porcelain vases and flowered tea- sets. At the door of the stall a young lady was talking and laughing with two young gentlemen. I remarked their English accents and listened vaguely to their conversation.

"O, I never said such a thing!"

"O, but you did!"

"O, but I didn't!"

"Didn't she say that?"

"Yes. I heard her."

"O, there's a ... fib!"

Observing me the young lady came over and asked me did I wish to buy anything. The tone of her voice was not encouraging; she seemed to have spoken to me out of a sense of duty. I looked humbly at the great jars that stood like eastern guards at either side of the dark

entrance to the stall and murmured:

"No, thank you."

The young lady changed the position of one of the vases and went back to the two young men. They began to talk of the same subject. Once or twice the young lady glanced at me over her shoulder.

I lingered before her stall, though I knew my stay was useless, to make my interest in her wares seem the more real. Then I turned away slowly and walked down the middle of the bazaar. I allowed the two pennies to fall against the sixpence in my pocket. I heard a voice call from one end of the gallery that the light was out. The upper part of the hall was now completely dark.

Gazing up into the darkness I saw myself as a creature driven and derided by vanity; and my eyes burned with anguish and anger.

Fin

Extracts From Adam's Diary

Mark Twain

MONDAY -- This new creature with the long hair is a good deal in the way. It is always hanging around and following me about. I don't like this; I am not used to company. I wish it would stay with the other animals. . . . Cloudy today, wind in the east; think we shall have rain. . . . WE? Where did I get that word-the new creature uses it.

TUESDAY -- Been examining the great waterfall. It is the finest thing on the estate, I think. The new creature calls it Niagara Falls-why, I am sure I do not know. Says it LOOKS like Niagara Falls. That is not a reason, it is mere waywardness and imbecility. I get no chance to name anything myself. The new creature names everything that comes along, before I can get in a protest. And always that same pretext is offered -- it LOOKS like the thing. There is a dodo, for instance. Says the moment one looks at it one sees at a glance that it "looks like a dodo." It will have to keep that name, no doubt. It wearies me to fret about it, and it does no good, anyway. Dodo! It looks no more like a dodo than I do.

WEDNESDAY -- Built me a shelter against the rain, but could not have it to myself in peace. The new creature intruded. When I tried to put it out it shed water out of the holes it looks with, and wiped it away with the back of its paws, and made a noise such as some of the other animals make when they are in distress. I wish it would not talk; it is always talking. That sounds like a cheap fling at the poor creature, a slur; but I do not mean it so. I have never heard the human voice before, and any new and strange sound intruding itself here upon the solemn hush of these dreaming solitudes offends my ear and seems a false note. And this new sound is so close to me; it is right at my shoulder, right at my ear, first on one side and then on the other, and I am used only to sounds that are more or less distant from me.

FRIDAY -- The naming goes recklessly on, in spite of anything I can do. I had a very good name for the estate, and it was musical and pretty -- GARDEN OF EDEN. Privately, I continue to call it that, but not any longer publicly. The new creature says it is all woods and rocks and scenery, and therefore has no resemblance to a garden. Says it LOOKS like a park, and does not look like anything BUT a park. Consequently, without consulting me, it has been new-named NIAGARA FALLS PARK. This is sufficiently high-handed, it seems to me. And already there is a sign up:

KEEP OFF THE GRASS

My life is not as happy as it was.

SATURDAY -- The new creature eats too much fruit. We are going to run short, most likely. "We" again -- that is ITS word; mine, too, now, from hearing it so much. Good deal of fog this morning. I do not go out in the fog myself. This new creature does. It goes out in all weathers, and stumps right in with its muddy feet. And talks. It used to be so pleasant and quiet here.

SUNDAY -- Pulled through. This day is getting to be more and more trying. It was selected and set apart last November as a day of rest. I had already six of them per week before. This morning found the new creature trying to clod apples out of that forbidden tree.

MONDAY -- The new creature says its name is Eve. That is all right, I have no objections. Says it is to call it by, when I want it to come. I said it was superfluous, then. The word evidently raised me in its respect; and indeed it is a large, good word and will bear repetition. It says it is not an It, it is a She. This is probably doubtful; yet it is all one to me; what she is were nothing to me if she would but go by herself and not talk.

TUESDAY -- She has littered the whole estate with execrable names and offensive signs:

This way to the Whirlpool
This way to Goat Island
Cave of the Winds this way

She says this park would make a tidy summer resort if there was any custom for it. Summer resort -- another invention of hers-just words, without any meaning. What is a summer resort? But it is best not to ask her, she has such a rage for explaining.

FRIDAY -- She has taken to beseeching me to stop going over the Falls. What harm does it do? Says it makes her shudder. I wonder why; I have always done it -- always liked the plunge, and coolness. I supposed it was what the Falls were for. They have no other use that I can see, and they must have been made for something. She says they were only made for scenery -- like the rhinoceros and the mastodon.

I went over the Falls in a barrel -- not satisfactory to her. Went over in a tub -- still not satisfactory. Swam the Whirlpool and the Rapids in a fig-leaf suit. It got much damaged. Hence, tedious complaints about my extravagance. I am too much hampered here. What I need is a change of scene.

SATURDAY -- I escaped last Tuesday night, and traveled two days, and built me another shelter in a secluded place, and obliterated my tracks as well as I could, but she hunted me out by means of a beast which she has tamed and calls a wolf, and came making that pitiful noise again, and shedding that water out of the places she looks with. I was obliged to return with her, but will presently emigrate again when occasion offers. She engages herself in many foolish things; among others; to study out why the animals called lions and tigers live on grass and flowers, when, as she says, the sort of teeth they wear would indicate that they were intended to eat each other. This is foolish, because to do that would be to kill each other, and that would introduce what, as I understand, is called "death"; and death, as I have been told, has not yet entered the Park. Which is a pity, on some accounts.

SUNDAY -- Pulled through.

MONDAY -- I believe I see what the week is for: it is to give time to rest up from the weariness of Sunday. It seems a good idea. . . . She has been climbing that tree again. Clodded her out of it. She said nobody was looking. Seems to consider that a sufficient justification for chancing any dangerous thing. Told her that. The word justification moved her admiration -- and envy, too, I thought. It is a good word.

TUESDAY -- She told me she was made out of a rib taken from my body. This is at least doubtful, if not more than that. I have not missed any rib. . . . She is in much trouble about the buzzard; says grass does not agree with it; is afraid she can't raise it; thinks it was intended to live on decayed flesh. The buzzard must get along the best it can with what is provided. We cannot overturn the whole scheme to accommodate the buzzard.

SATURDAY -- She fell in the pond yesterday when she was looking at herself in it, which she is always doing. She nearly strangled, and said it was most uncomfortable. This made her sorry for the creatures which live in there, which she calls fish, for she continues to fasten names on to things that don't need them and don't come when they are called by them, which is a matter of no consequence to her, she is such a numbskull, anyway; so she got a lot of them out and brought them in last night and put them in my bed to keep warm, but I have noticed them now and then all day and I don't see that they are any happier there then they were before, only quieter. When night comes I shall throw them outdoors. I will not sleep with them again, for I find them clammy and unpleasant to lie among when a person hasn't anything on.

SUNDAY -- Pulled through.

TUESDAY -- She has taken up with a snake now. The other animals are glad, for she was always experimenting with them and bothering them; and I am glad because the snake talks, and this enables me to get a rest.

FRIDAY -- She says the snake advises her to try the fruit of the tree, and says the result will be a great and fine and noble education. I told her there would be another result, too -- it would introduce death into the world. That was a mistake -- it had been better to keep the remark to myself; it only gave her an idea --

she could save the sick buzzard, and furnish fresh meat to the despondent lions and tigers. I advised her to keep away from the tree. She said she wouldn't. I foresee trouble. Will emigrate.

WEDNESDAY -- I have had a variegated time. I escaped last night, and rode a horse all night as fast as he could go, hoping to get clear of the Park and hide in some other country before the trouble should begin; but it was not to be. About an hour after sun-up, as I was riding through a flowery plain where thousands of animals were grazing, slumbering, or playing with each other, according to their wont, all of a sudden they broke into a tempest of frightful noises, and in one moment the plain was a frantic commotion and every beast was destroying its neighbor. I knew what it meant-Eve had eaten that fruit, and death was come into the world. . . . The tigers ate my house, paying no attention when I ordered them to desist, and they would have eaten me if I had stayed-which I didn't, but went away in much haste. . . . I found this place, outside the Park, and was fairly comfortable for a few days, but she has found me out. Found me out, and has named the place Tonawanda-says it LOOKS like that. In fact I was not sorry she came, for there are but meager pickings here, and she brought some of those apples. I was obliged to eat them, I was so hungry. It was against my principles, but I find that principles have no real force except when one is well fed. . . . She came curtained in boughs and bunches of leaves, and when I asked her what she meant by such nonsense, and snatched them away and threw them down, she tittered and blushed. I had never seen a person titter and blush before, and to me it seemed unbecoming and idiotic. She said I would soon know how it was myself. This was correct. Hungry as I was, I laid down the apple half-eaten -- certainly the best one I ever saw, considering the lateness of the season-and arrayed myself in the discarded boughs and branches, and then spoke to her with some severity and ordered her to go and get some more and not make a spectacle or herself. She did it, and after this we crept down to where the wild-beast battle had been, and collected some skins, and I made her patch together a couple of suits proper for public occasions. They are uncomfortable, it is true, but stylish, and that is the main point about clothes. . . . I find she is a good deal of a companion. I see I should be lonesome and depressed without her, now that I have lost my property. Another thing, she says it is ordered that we work for our living hereafter. She will be useful. I will superintend.

TEN DAYS LATER -- She accuses ME of being the cause of our disaster! She says, with apparent sincerity and truth, that the Serpent assured her that the forbidden fruit was not apples, it was chestnuts. I said I was innocent, then, for I had not eaten any chestnuts. She said the Serpent informed her that "chestnut" was a figurative term meaning an aged and moldy joke. I turned pale at that, for I have made many jokes to pass the weary time, and some of them could have been of that sort, though I had honestly supposed that they were new when I made them. She asked me if I had made one just at the time of the catastrophe. I was obliged to admit that I had made one to myself, though not aloud. It was this. I was thinking about the Falls, and I said to myself, "How wonderful it is to see that vast body of water tumble down there!" Then in an instant a bright thought flashed into my head, and I let it fly, saying, "It would be a deal more wonderful to see it tumble UP there!" -- and I was just about to kill myself with laughing at it when all nature broke loose in war and death and I had to flee for my life. "There," she said, with triumph, "that is just it; the Serpent mentioned that very jest, and called it the First Chestnut, and said it was coeval with the creation." Alas, I am indeed to blame. Would that I were not witty; oh, that I had never had that radiant thought!

NEXT YEAR -- We have named it Cain. She caught it while I was up country trapping on the North Shore of the Erie; caught it in the timber a couple of miles from our dug-out -- or it might have been four, she isn't certain which. It resembles us in some ways, and may be a relation. That is what she thinks, but this is an error, in my judgment. The difference in size warrants the conclusion that it is a different and new kind of animal -- a fish, perhaps, though when I put it in the water to see, it sank, and she plunged in and snatched it out before there was opportunity for the experiment to determine the matter. I still think it is a fish, but she is indifferent about what it is, and will not let me have it to try. I do not understand this. The coming of the creature seems to have changed her whole nature and made her unreasonable about experiments. She thinks more of it than she does of any of the other animals, but is not able to explain why. Her mind is disordered -- everything shows it. Sometimes she carries the fish in her arms half the night when it complains and wants to get to the water. At such times the water comes out of the places in her face that she looks out of, and she pats the fish on the back and makes soft sounds with her mouth to soothe it, and betrays sorrow and solicitude in a hundred ways. I have never seen her do like this with any other fish, and it troubles me greatly. She used to carry the young tigers around so, and play with them, before we lost our property, but it was only play; she never took on about them like this when their dinner disagreed with them.

SUNDAY -- She doesn't work, Sundays, but lies around all tired out, and likes to have the fish wallow over her; and she makes fool noises to amuse it, and pretends to chew its paws, and that makes it laugh. I have not seen a fish before that could laugh. This makes me doubt. . . . I have come to like Sunday myself. Superintending all the week tires a body so. There ought to be more Sundays. In the old days they were tough, but now they come handy.

WEDNESDAY -- It isn't a fish. I cannot quite make out what it is. It makes curious devilish noises when not satisfied, and says "goo-goo" when it is. It is not one of us, for it doesn't walk; it is not a bird, for it doesn't fly; it is not a frog, for it doesn't hop; it is not a snake, for it doesn't crawl; I feel sure it is not a fish, though I cannot get a chance to find out whether it can swim or not. It merely lies around, and mostly on its back, with its feet up. I have not seen any other animal do that before. I said I believed it was an enigma; but she only admired the word without understanding it. In my judgment it is either an enigma or some king of a bug. If it dies, I will take it apart and see what its arrangements are. I never had a thing perplex me so.

THREE MONTHS LATER -- The perplexity augments instead of diminishing. I sleep but little. It has ceased from lying around, and goes about on its four legs now. Yet it differs from the other four legged animals, in that its front legs are unusually short, consequently this causes the main part of its person to stick up uncomfortably high in the air, and this is not attractive. It is built much as we are, but its method of traveling shows that it is not of our breed.

The short front legs and long hind ones indicate that it is a of the kangaroo family, but it is a marked variation of that species, since the true kangaroo hops, whereas this one never does. Still it is a curious and interesting variety, and has not been catalogued before. As I discovered it, I have felt justified in securing the credit of the discovery by attaching my name to it, and hence have called it KANGAROORUM ADAMIENSIS. . . . It must have been a young one when it came, for it has grown exceedingly since. It must be five times as big, now, as it was then, and when discontented it is able to make from twenty-two to thirty-eight times the noise it made at first. Coercion does not modify this, but has the contrary effect. For this reason I discontinued the system. She reconciles it by persuasion, and by giving it things which she had previously told me she wouldn't give it. As already observed, I was not at home when it first came, and she told me she found it in the woods. It seems odd that it should be the only one, yet it must be so, for I have worn myself out these many weeks trying to find another one to add to my collection, and for this to play with; for surely then it would be quieter and we could tame it more easily. But I find none, nor any vestige of any; and strangest of all, no tracks. It has to live on the ground, it cannot help itself; therefore, how does it get about without leaving a track? I have set a dozen traps, but they do no good. I catch all small animals except that one; animals that merely go into the trap out of curiosity, I think, to see what the milk is there for. They never drink it.

THREE MONTHS LATER -- The Kangaroo still continues to grow, which is very strange and perplexing. I never knew one to be so long getting its growth. It has fur on its head now; not like kangaroo fur, but exactly like our hair except that it is much finer and softer, and instead of being black is red. I am like to lose my mind over the capricious and harassing developments of this unclassifiable zoological freak. If I could catch another one -- but that is hopeless; it is a new variety, and the only sample; this is plain. But I caught a true kangaroo and brought it in, thinking that this one, being lonesome, would rather have that for company than have no kin at all, or any animal it could feel a nearness to or get sympathy from in its forlorn condition here among strangers who do not know its ways or habits, or what to do to make it feel that it is among friends; but it was a mistake -- it went into such fits at the sight of the kangaroo that I was convinced it had never seen one before. I pity the poor noisy little animal, but there is nothing I can do to make it happy. If I could tame it -- but that is out of the question; the more I try the worse I seem to make it. It grieves me to the heart to see it in its little storms of sorrow and passion. I wanted to let it go, but she wouldn't hear of it. That seemed cruel and not like her; and yet she may be right. It might be lonelier than ever; for since I cannot find another one, how could IT?

FIVE MONTHS LATER -- It is not a kangaroo. No, for it supports itself by holding to her finger, and thus goes a few steps on its hind legs, and then falls down. It is probably some kind of a bear; and yet it has no tail -- as yet -- and no fur, except upon its head. It still keeps on growing -- that is a curious circumstance, for bears get their growth earlier than this. Bears are dangerous-since our catastrophe -- and I shall not be satisfied to have this one prowling about the place much longer without a muzzle on. I have offered to get her a kangaroo if she would let this one go, but it did no good -- she is determined to run us into all sorts of foolish risks, I think. She was not like this before she lost her mind.

A FORTNIGHT LATER -- I examined its mouth. There is no danger yet: it has only one tooth. It has no tail yet. It makes more noise now than it ever did before -- and mainly at night. I have moved out. But I shall go over, mornings, to breakfast, and see if it has more teeth. If it gets a mouthful of teeth it will be time for it to go, tail or no tail, for a bear does not need a tail in order to be dangerous.

FOUR MONTHS LATER -- I have been off hunting and fishing a month, up in the region that she calls Buffalo; I don't know why, unless it is because there are not any buffaloes there. Meantime the bear has learned to paddle around all by itself on its hind legs, and says "poppa" and "momma." It is certainly a new species. This resemblance to words may be purely accidental, of course, and may have no purpose or meaning; but even in that case it is still extraordinary, and is a thing which no other bear can do. This imitation of speech, taken together with general absence of fur and entire absence of tail, sufficiently indicates that this is a new kind of bear. The further study of it will be exceedingly interesting. Meantime I will go off on a far expedition among the forests of the north and make an exhaustive search. There must certainly be another one somewhere, and this one will be less dangerous when it has company of its own species. I will go straightway; but I will muzzle this one first.

THREE MONTHS LATER -- It has been a weary, weary hunt, yet I have had no success. In the mean time, without stirring from the home estate, she has caught another one! I never saw such luck. I might have hunted these woods a hundred years, I never would have run across that thing.

NEXT DAY -- I have been comparing the new one with the old one, and it is perfectly plain that they are of the same breed. I was going to stuff one of them for my collection, but she is prejudiced against it for some reason or other; so I have relinquished the idea, though I think it is a mistake. It would be an irreparable loss to science if they should get away. The old one is tamer than it was and can laugh and talk like a parrot, having learned this, no doubt, from being with the parrot so much, and having the imitative faculty in a high developed degree. I shall be astonished if it turns out to be a new kind of parrot; and yet I ought not to be astonished, for it has already been everything else it could think of since those first days when it was a fish. The new one is as ugly as the old one was at first; has the same sulphur-and-raw-meat complexion and the same singular head without any fur on it. She calls it Abel.

TEN YEARS LATER -- They are BOYS; we found it out long ago. It was their coming in that small immature shape that puzzled us; we were not used to it. There are some girls now. Abel is a good boy, but if Cain had stayed a bear it would have improved him. After all these years, I see that I was mistaken about Eve in the beginning; it is better to live outside the Garden with her than inside it without her. At first I thought she talked too much; but now I should be sorry to have that voice fall silent and pass out of my life. Blessed be the chestnut that brought us near together and taught me to know the goodness of her heart and the sweetness of her spirit!

fin

Daredevil Joins Tanks

Ernest Hemingway

"Have you ever had any gas engine experience?" asked Lieut. Frank E. Cooter, special tank officer at the army recruiting station, Twelfth Street and Grand Avenue, yesterday.

"Well, you might call it that," replied William A. Whitman, 914 East Ninth Street. "I've driven a Blitzen-Benz at the Chicago, New York, Cincinnati and Los Angeles speedways for the last four years. You might call my race with Ralph Mulford at Reno a gas engine experience. Or the time the old boat got up to 111 miles an hour at the Sheepshead Bay track, or when Bob Burman was killed on the big board oval and I piled up right behind him. Those were gas engine experiences."

"But have you had any military experience?" asked Lieutenant Cooter.

"Well, not regular military. I held a lieutenant's commission in the Nicaraugan army in the war against

Honduras in 1909. I was also a machine gun captain with Madero when he put Diaz out. First American to get into Juarez. Ask Pancho Villa, he knows . But none of those were very military. I had a commission in a couple of Central American revolutions, too. Nothing very military there, either."

Lieutenant Cooter shoved a blank toward him. "Sign on the dotted line, man," he said. "You're too good to be true!"

"Well, I haven't raced since September at Sheepshead Bay, and I may be a little out of practice, but you don't have to go so fast in a tank. Besides, I've got a little difficulty with my teeth. But I sure want to sign for the tanks."

Lieutenant Cooter has wired Washington requesting waivers as to the teeth.

Besides the regular quota of mechanics, barbers, motor car salesmen, bartenders and college students who applied yesterday, Maynard Bush, 38 years old, instructor in journalism at Polytechnic Junior College, made out an application. He will not be enlisted until next week, so he may arrange for a successor.

Letters were received from several Kansas University students who wish to enter. The Sigma Alpha Epsilon

Chapter at Manhattan, Kas., wrote that several of its members wished to enlist. Telegrams and letters came throughout yesterday in regard to the t ank service.

One hundred and sixteen men were accepted by Lieutenant Cooter during the week for immediate service. Nineteen were taken yesterday.

—30—

The Allegory of the Cave, from The Republic

Plato

[Socrates] And now, I said, let me show in a figure how far our nature is enlightened or unenlightened: -- Behold! human beings living in a underground cave, which has a mouth open towards the light and reaching all along the cave; here they have been from their childhood, and have their legs and necks chained so that they cannot move, and can only see before them, being prevented by the chains from turning round their heads. Above and behind them a fire is blazing at a distance, and between the fire and the prisoners there is a raised way; and you will see, if you look, a low wall built along the way, like the screen which marionette players have in front of them, over which they show the puppets.

[Glaucon] I see.

[Socrates] And do you see, I said, men passing along the wall carrying all sorts of vessels, and statues and figures of animals made of wood and stone and various materials, which appear over the wall? Some of them are talking, others silent.

[Glaucon] You have shown me a strange image, and they are strange prisoners.

[Socrates] Like ourselves, I replied; and they see only their own shadows, or the shadows of one another, which the fire throws on the opposite wall of the cave?

[Glaucon] True, he said; how could they see anything but the shadows if they were never allowed to move their heads?

[Socrates] And of the objects which are being carried in like manner they would only see the shadows?

[Glaucon] Yes, he said.

[Socrates] And if they were able to converse with one another, would they not suppose that they were naming what was actually before them?

[Glaucon] Very true.

[Socrates] And suppose further that the prison had an echo which came from the other side, would they not be sure to fancy when one of the passers-by spoke that the voice which they heard came from the passing shadow?

[Glaucon] No question, he replied.

[Socrates] To them, I said, the truth would be literally nothing but the shadows of the images.

[Glaucon] That is certain.

[Socrates] And now look again, and see what will naturally follow if the prisoners are released and disabused of their error. At first, when any of them is liberated and compelled suddenly to stand up and turn his neck round and walk and look towards the light, he will suffer sharp pains; the glare will distress him, and he will be unable to see the realities of which in his former state he had seen the shadows; and then conceive some one saying to him, that what he saw before was an illusion, but that now, when he is approaching nearer to being and his eye is turned towards more real existence, he has a clearer vision, - what will be his reply? And you may further imagine that his instructor is pointing to the objects as they pass and requiring him to name them, -will he not be perplexed? Will he not fancy that the shadows which he formerly saw are truer than the objects which are now shown to him?

[Glaucon] Far truer.

[Socrates] And if he is compelled to look straight at the light, will he not have a pain in his eyes which will make him turn away to take and take in the objects of vision which he can see, and which he will conceive to be in reality clearer than the things which are now being shown to him?

[Glaucon] True, he now.

[Socrates] And suppose once more, that he is reluctantly dragged up a steep and rugged ascent, and held fast until he 's forced into the presence of the sun himself, is he not likely to be pained and irritated? When he approaches the light his eyes will be dazzled, and he will not be able to see anything at all of what are now called realities.

[Glaucon] Not all in a moment, he said.

[Socrates] He will require to grow accustomed to the sight of the upper world. And first he will see the shadows best, next the reflections of men and other objects in the water, and then the objects themselves; then he will gaze upon the light of the moon and the stars and the spangled heaven; and he will see the sky and the stars by night better than the sun or the light of the sun by day?

[Glaucon] Certainly.

[Socrates] Last of he will be able to see the sun, and not mere reflections of him in the water, but he will see him in his own proper place, and not in another; and he will contemplate him as he is.

[Glaucon] Certainly.

[Socrates] He will then proceed to argue that this is he who gives the season and the years, and is the guardian of all that is in the visible world, and in a certain way the cause of all things which he and his fellows have been accustomed to behold?

[Glaucon] Clearly, he said, he would first see the sun and then reason about him.

[Socrates] And when he remembered his old habitation, and the wisdom of the cave and his fellow-prisoners, do you not suppose that he would felicitate himself on the change, and pity them?

[Glaucon] Certainly, he would.

[Socrates] And if they were in the habit of conferring honors among themselves on those who were quickest to observe the passing shadows and to remark which of them went before, and which followed after, and which were together; and who were therefore best able to draw conclusions as to the future, do you think that he would care for such honors and glories, or envy the possessors of them? Would he not say with Homer, Better to be the poor servant of a poor master, and to endure anything, rather than think as they do and live after their manner?

[Glaucon] Yes, he said, I think that he would rather suffer anything than entertain these false

notions and live in this miserable manner.

[Socrates] Imagine once more, I said, such an one coming suddenly out of the sun to be replaced in his old situation; would he not be certain to have his eyes full of darkness?

[Glaucon] To be sure, he said.

[Socrates] And if there were a contest, and he had to compete in measuring the shadows with the prisoners who had never moved out of the cave, while his sight was still weak, and before his eyes had become steady (and the time which would be needed to acquire this new habit of sight might be very considerable) would he not be ridiculous? Men would say of him that up he went and down he came without his eyes; and that it was better not even to think of ascending; and if any one tried to loose another and lead him up to the light, let them only catch the offender, and they would put him to death.

[Glaucon] No question, he said.

[Socrates] This entire allegory, I said, you may now append, dear Glaucon, to the previous argument; the prison-house is the world of sight, the light of the fire is the sun, and you will not misapprehend me if you interpret the journey upwards to be the ascent of the soul into the intellectual world according to my poor belief, which, at your desire, I have expressed whether rightly or wrongly God knows. But, whether true or false, my opinion is that in the world of knowledge the idea of good appears last of all, and is seen only with an effort; and, when seen, is also inferred to be the universal author of all things beautiful and right, parent of light and of the lord of light in this visible world, and the immediate source of reason and truth in the intellectual; and that this is the power upon which he who would act rationally, either in public or private life must have his eye fixed.

[Glaucon] I agree, he said, as far as I am able to understand you.

[Socrates] Moreover, I said, you must not wonder that those who attain to this beatific vision are unwilling to descend to human affairs; for their souls are ever hastening into the upper world where they desire to dwell; which desire of theirs is very natural, if our allegory may be trusted.

[Glaucon] Yes, very natural.

[Socrates] And is there anything surprising in one who passes from divine contemplations to the evil state of man, misbehaving himself in a ridiculous manner; if, while his eyes are blinking and before he has become accustomed to the surrounding darkness, he is compelled to fight in courts of law, or in other places, about the images or the shadows of images of justice, and is endeavoring to meet the conceptions of those who have never yet seen absolute justice?

[Glaucon] Anything but surprising, he replied.

[Socrates] Any one who has common sense will remember that the bewilderments of the eyes are of two kinds, and arise from two causes, either from coming out of the light or from going into the light, which is true of the mind's eye, quite as much as of the bodily eye; and he who remembers this when he sees any one whose vision is perplexed and weak, will not be too ready to laugh; he will first ask whether that soul of man has come out of the brighter light, and is unable to see because unaccustomed to the dark, or having turned from darkness to the day is dazzled by excess of light. And he will count the one happy in his condition and state of being, and he will pity the other; or, if he have a mind to laugh at the soul which comes from below into the light, there will be more reason in this than in the laugh which greets him who returns from above out of the light into the cave.

[Glaucon] That, he said, is a very just distinction.

[Socrates] But then, if I am right, certain professors of education must be wrong when they say that they can put a knowledge into the soul which was not there before, like sight into blind eyes.

[Glaucon] They undoubtedly say this, he replied.

[Socrates] Whereas, our argument shows that the power and capacity of learning exists in the soul already; and that just as the eye was unable to turn from darkness to light without the whole body, so too the instrument of knowledge can only by the movement of the whole soul be turned

from the world of becoming into that of being, and learn by degrees to endure the sight of being, and of the brightest and best of being, or in other words, of the good.

[Glaucon] Very true.

[Socrates] And must there not be some art which will effect conversion in the easiest and quickest manner; not implanting the faculty of sight, for that exists already, but has been turned in the wrong direction, and is looking away from the truth?

[Glaucon] Yes, he said, such an art may be presumed.

[Socrates] And whereas the other so-called virtues of the soul seem to be akin to bodily qualities, for even when they are not originally innate they can be implanted later by habit and exercise, the of wisdom more than anything else contains a divine element which always remains, and by this conversion is rendered useful and profitable; or, on the other hand, hurtful and useless. Did you never observe the narrow intelligence flashing from the keen eye of a clever rogue --how eager he is, how clearly his paltry soul sees the way to his end; he is the reverse of blind, but his keen eyesight is forced into the service of evil, and he is mischievous in proportion to his cleverness.

[Glaucon] Very true, he said.

[Socrates] But what if there had been a circumcision of such natures in the days of their youth; and they had been severed from those sensual pleasures, such as eating and drinking, which, like leaden weights, were attached to them at their birth, and which drag them down and turn the vision of their souls upon the things that are below --if, I say, they had been released from these impediments and turned in the opposite direction, the very same faculty in them would have seen the truth as keenly as they see what their eyes are turned to now.

[Glaucon] Very likely.

[Socrates] Yes, I said; and there is another thing which is likely. or rather a necessary inference from what has preceded, that neither the uneducated and uninformed of the truth, nor yet those who never make an end of their education, will be able ministers of State; not the former, because they have no single aim of duty which is the rule of all their actions, private as well as public; nor the latter, because they will not act at all except upon compulsion, fancying that they are already dwelling apart in the islands of the blest.

[Glaucon] Very true, he replied.

[Socrates] Then, I said, the business of us who are the founders of the State will be to compel the best minds to attain that knowledge which we have already shown to be the greatest of all-they must continue to ascend until they arrive at the good; but when they have ascended and seen enough we must not allow them to do as they do now.

[Glaucon] What do you mean?

[Socrates] I mean that they remain in the upper world: but this must not be allowed; they must be made to descend again among the prisoners in the cave, and partake of their labors and honors, whether they are worth having or not.

[Glaucon] But is not this unjust? he said; ought we to give them a worse life, when they might have a better?

[Socrates] You have again forgotten, my friend, I said, the intention of the legislator, who did not aim at making any one class in the State happy above the rest; the happiness was to be in the whole State, and he held the citizens together by persuasion and necessity, making them benefactors of the State, and therefore benefactors of one another; to this end he created them, not to please themselves, but to be his instruments in binding up the State.

[Glaucon] True, he said, I had forgotten.

[Socrates] Observe, Glaucon, that there will be no injustice in compelling our philosophers to have a care and providence of others; we shall explain to them that in other States, men of their class are not obliged to share in the toils of politics: and this is reasonable, for they grow up at their own sweet will, and the government would rather not have them. Being self-taught, they cannot be expected to show any gratitude for a culture which they have never received. But we have brought you into the world to be rulers of the hive, kings of yourselves and of the other citizens, and have educated you far better and more perfectly than they have been educated, and you are better able to share in the double duty. Wherefore each of you, when his turn comes, must go down to the general underground abode, and get the habit of seeing in the dark. When you have acquired the habit, you will see ten thousand times better than the inhabitants of the cave, and you will know what the several images are, and what they represent, because you have seen the beautiful and just and good in their truth. And thus our State which is also yours will be a reality, and not a dream only, and will be administered in a spirit unlike that of other States, in which men fight with one another about shadows only and are distracted in the struggle for power, which in their eyes is a great good. Whereas the truth is that the State in which the rulers are most reluctant to govern is always the best and most quietly governed, and the State in which they are most eager, the worst.

[Glaucon] Quite true, he replied.

[Socrates] And will our pupils, when they hear this, refuse to take their turn at the toils of State, when they are allowed to spend the greater part of their time with one another in the heavenly light?

[Glaucon] Impossible, he answered; for they are just men, and the commands which we impose upon them are just; there can be no doubt that every one of them will take office as a stern necessity, and not after the fashion of our present rulers of State.

[Socrates] Yes, my friend, I said; and there lies the point. You must contrive for your future rulers another and a better life than that of a ruler, and then you may have a well-ordered State; for only in the State which offers this, will they rule who are truly rich, not in silver and gold, but in virtue and wisdom, which are the true blessings of life. Whereas if they go to the administration of public affairs, poor and hungering after the' own private advantage, thinking that hence they are to snatch the chief good, order there can never be; for they will be fighting about office, and the civil and domestic broils which thus arise will be the ruin of the rulers themselves and of the whole State.

[Glaucon] Most true, he replied.

[Socrates] And the only life which looks down upon the life of political ambition is that of true philosophy. Do you know of any other?

[Glaucon] Indeed, I do not, he said.

[Socrates] And those who govern ought not to be lovers of the task? For, if they are, there will be rival lovers, and they will fight.

[Glaucon] No question.

[Socrates] Who then are those whom we shall compel to be guardians? Surely they will be the men who are wisest about affairs of State, and by whom the State is best administered, and who at the same time have other honors and another and a better life than that of politics?

[Glaucon] They are the men, and I will choose them, he replied.

[Socrates] And now shall we consider in what way such guardians will be produced, and how they are to be brought from darkness to light, -- as some are said to have ascended from the world below to the gods?

[Glaucon] By all means, he replied.

[Socrates] The process, I said, is not the turning over of an oyster-shell, but the turning round of a soul passing from a day which is little better than night to the true day of being, that is, the ascent from below, which we affirm to be true philosophy?

[Glaucon] Quite so.

fin

F Scott Fitzgerald

THE JELLY-BEAN.

Jim Powell was a Jelly-bean. Much as I desire to make him an appealing
character, I feel that it would be unscrupulous to deceive you on that
point. He was a bred-in-the-bone, dyed-in-the-wool, ninety-nine
three-quarters per cent Jelly-bean and he grew lazily all during
Jelly-bean season, which is every season, down in the land of the
Jelly-beans well below the Mason-Dixon line.

Now if you call a Memphis man a Jelly-bean he will quite possibly pull
a long sinewy rope from his hip pocket and hang you to a convenient
telegraph-pole. If you Call a New Orleans man a Jelly-bean he will
probably grin and ask you who is taking your girl to the Mardi Gras

ball. The particular Jelly-bean patch which produced the protagonist
of this history lies somewhere between the two--a little city of forty
thousand that has dozed sleepily for forty thousand years in southern
Georgia occasionally stirring in its slumbers and muttering something
about a war that took place sometime, somewhere, and that everyone
else has forgotten long ago.

Jim was a Jelly-bean. I write that again because it has such a
pleasant sound--rather like the beginning of a fairy story--as if Jim
were nice. It somehow gives me a picture of him with a round,
appetizing face and all sort of leaves and vegetables growing out of
his cap. But Jim was long and thin and bent at the waist from stooping
over pool-tables, and he was what might have been known in the
indiscriminating North as a corner loafer. "Jelly-bean" is the name

throughout the undissolved Confederacy for one who spends his life

conjugating the verb to idle in the first person singular--I am

idling, I have idled, I will idle.

Jim was born in a white house on a green corner, It had four

weather-beaten pillars in front and a great amount of lattice-work in

the rear that made a cheerful criss-cross background for a flowery

sun-drenched lawn. Originally the dwellers in the white house had

owned the ground next door and next door to that and next door to

that, but this had been so long ago that even Jim's father, scarcely

remembered it. He had, in fact, thought it a matter of so little

moment that when he was dying from a pistol wound got in a brawl he

neglected even to tell little Jim, who was five years old and

miserably frightened. The white house became a boarding-house run by a

tight-lipped lady from Macon, whom Jim called Aunt
Mamie and detested
with all his soul.

He became fifteen, went to high school, wore his hair
in black snarls,
and was afraid of girls. He hated his home where four
women and one
old man prolonged an interminable chatter from
summer to summer about
what lots the Powell place had originally included
and what sorts of
flowers would be out next. Sometimes the parents of
little girls in
town, remembering Jim's mother and fancying a
resemblance in the dark
eyes and hair, invited him to parties, but parties made
him shy and he
much preferred sitting on a disconnected axle in
Tilly's Garage,
rolling the bones or exploring his mouth endlessly
with a long straw.
For pocket money, he picked up odd jobs, and it was
due to this that
he stopped going to parties. At his third party little
Marjorie Haight

had whispered indiscreetly and within hearing distance that he was a
boy who brought the groceries sometimes. So instead of the two-step
and polka, Jim had learned to throw, any number he desired on the dice
and had listened to spicy tales of all the shootings that had occurred
in the surrounding country during the past fifty years.

He became eighteen. The war broke out and he enlisted as a gob and
polished brass in the Charleston Navy-yard for a year. Then, by way of
variety, he went North and polished brass in the Brooklyn Navy-yard
for a year.

When the war was over he came home, He was twenty-one, has trousers
were too short and too tight. His buttoned shoes were long and narrow.
His tie was an alarming conspiracy of purple and pink marvellously
scrolled, and over it were two blue eyes faded like a piece of very

good old cloth, long exposed to the sun.

In the twilight of one April evening when a soft gray
had drifted down
along the cottonfields and over the sultry town, he
was a vague figure
leaning against a board fence, whistling and gazing at
the moon's rim
above the lights of Jackson Street. His mind was
working persistently
on a problem that had held his attention for an hour.
The Jelly-bean had
been invited to a party.

Back in the days when all the boys had detested all
the girls, Clark
Darrow and Jim had sat side by side in school. But,
while Jim's social
aspirations had died in the oily air of the garage,
Clark had
alternately fallen in and out of love, gone to college,
taken to
drink, given it up, and, in short, become one of the
best beaux of the
town. Nevertheless Clark and Jim had retained a
friendship that,

though casual, was perfectly definite. That afternoon Clark's ancient
Ford had slowed up beside Jim, who was on the sidewalk and, out of a
clear sky, Clark invited him to a party at the country club. The
impulse that made him do this was no stranger than the impulse which
made Jim accept. The latter was probably an unconscious ennui, a
half-frightened sense of adventure. And now Jim was soberly thinking
it over.

He began to sing, drumming his long foot idly on a stone block in the
sidewalk till it wobbled up and down in time to the low throaty tune:

"One smile from Home in Jelly-bean town,
Lives Jeanne, the Jelly-bean Queen.
She loves her dice and treats 'em nice;
No dice would treat her mean."

He broke off and agitated the sidewalk to a bumpy gallop.

"Daggone!" he muttered, half aloud. They would all be there--the old

crowd, the crowd to which, by right of the white house, sold long

since, and the portrait of the officer in gray over the mantel, Jim

should have belonged. But that crowd had grown up together into a

tight little set as gradually as the girls' dresses had lengthened

inch by inch, as definitely as the boys' trousers had dropped suddenly

to their ankles. And to that society of first names and dead puppy

loves Jim was an outsider--a running mate of poor whites. Most of the

men knew him, condescendingly; he tipped his hat to three or four

girls. That was all.

When the dusk had thickened into a blue setting for the moon, he

walked through the hot, pleasantly pungent town to Jackson Street. The stores were closing and the last shoppers were drifting homeward, as

if borne on the dreamy revolution of a slow merry-go-round. A

street-fair farther down a brilliant alley of varicolored booths

contributed a blend of music to the night--an oriental dance on a

calliope, a melancholy bugle in front of a freak show, a cheerful

rendition of "Back Home in Tennessee" on a hand-organ.

The Jelly-bean stopped in a store and bought a collar. Then he

sauntered along toward Soda Sam's, where he found the usual three or

four cars of a summer evening parked in front and the little darkies

running back and forth with sundaes and lemonades.

"Hello, Jim."

It was a voice at his elbow--Joe Ewing sitting in an automobile with

Marylyn Wade. Nancy Lamar and a strange man were in the back seat.

The Jelly-bean tipped his hat quickly.

"Hi Ben--" then, after an almost imperceptible pause--"How y' all?"

Passing, he ambled on toward the garage where he had a room up-stairs.
His "How y'all" had been said to Nancy Lamar, to whom he had not
spoken in fifteen years.

Nancy had a mouth like a remembered kiss and shadowy eyes and
blue-black hair inherited from her mother who had been born in
Budapest. Jim passed her often on the street, walking small-boy
fashion with her hands in her pockets and he knew that with her
inseparable Sally Carrol Hopper she had left a trail of broken hearts
from Atlanta to New Orleans.

For a few fleeting moments Jim wished he could dance. Then he laughed
and as he reached his door began to sing softly to himself:

"Her Jelly Roll can twist your soul,
Her eyes are big and brown,
She's the Queen of the Queens of the Jelly-beans--
My Jeanne of Jelly-bean Town."

II

At nine-thirty, Jim and Clark met in front of Soda Sam's and started
for the Country Club in Clark's Ford. "Jim," asked Clark casually, as
they rattled through the jasmine-scented night, "how do you keep
alive?"

The Jelly-bean paused, considered.

"Well," he said finally, "I got a room over Tilly's garage. I help him some with the cars in the afternoon an' he gives it to me free.

Sometimes I drive one of his taxies and pick up a little thataway. I

get fed up doin' that regular though."

"That all?"

"Well, when there's a lot of work I help him by the day--Saturdays

usually--and then there's one main source of revenue I don't generally

mention. Maybe you don't recollect I'm about the champion crap-shooter

of this town. They make me shoot from a cup now because once I get the

feel of a pair of dice they just roll for me."

Clark grinned appreciatively,

"I never could learn to set 'em so's they'd do what I wanted. Wish

you'd shoot with Nancy Lamar some day and take all her money away from

her. She will roll 'em with the boys and she loses more than her daddy

can afford to give her. I happen to know she sold a good ring last
month to pay a debt."

The Jelly-bean was noncommittal.

"The white house on Elm Street still belong to you?"

Jim shook his head.

"Sold. Got a pretty good price, seein' it wasn't in a good part of
town no more. Lawyer told me to put it into Liberty bonds. But Aunt
Mamie got so she didn't have no sense, so it takes all the interest to
keep her up at Great Farms Sanitarium.

"Hm."

"I got an old uncle up-state an' I reckin I kin go up there if ever I
get sure enough pore. Nice farm, but not enough niggers around to work
it. He's asked me to come up and help him, but I don't guess I'd take

much to it. Too doggone lonesome--" He broke off suddenly. "Clark, I
want to tell you I'm much obliged to you for askin' me out, but I'd be
a lot happier if you'd just stop the car right here an' let me walk
back into town."

"Shucks!" Clark grunted. "Do you good to step out. You don't have to
dance--just get out there on the floor and shake."

"Hold on," exclaimed. Jim uneasily, "Don't you go leadin' me up to any
girls and leavin' me there so I'll have to dance with 'em."

Clark laughed.

"'Cause," continued Jim desperately, "without you swear you won't do
that I'm agoin' to get out right here an' my good legs goin' carry me
back to Jackson street."

They agreed after some argument that Jim,
unmolested by females, was
to view the spectacle from a secluded settee in the
corner where Clark
would join him whenever he wasn't dancing.

So ten o'clock found the Jelly-bean with his legs
crossed and his arms
conservatively folded, trying to look casually at home
and politely
uninterested in the dancers. At heart he was torn
between overwhelming
self-consciousness and an intense curiosity as to all
that went on
around him. He saw the girls emerge one by one from
the dressing-room,
stretching and pluming themselves like bright birds,
smiling over
their powdered shoulders at the chaperones, casting a
quick glance
around to take in the room and, simultaneously, the
room's reaction to
their entrance--and then, again like birds, alighting
and nestling in
the sober arms of their waiting escorts. Sally Carrol
Hopper, blonde

and lazy-eyed, appeared clad in her favorite pink and blinking like an

awakened rose. Marjorie Haight, Marylyn Wade, Harriet Cary, all the

girls he had seen loitering down Jackson Street by noon, now, curled

and brilliantined and delicately tinted for the overhead lights, were

miraculously strange Dresden figures of pink and blue and red and

gold, fresh from the shop and not yet fully dried.

He had been there half an hour, totally uncheered by Clark's jovial

visits which were each one accompanied by a "Hello, old boy, how you

making out?" and a slap at his knee. A dozen males had spoken to him

or stopped for a moment beside him, but he knew that they were each

one surprised at finding him there and fancied that one or two were

even slightly resentful. But at half past ten his embarrassment

suddenly left him and a pull of breathless interest took him

completely out of himself--Nancy Lamar had come out of the
dressing-room.

She was dressed in yellow organdie, a costume of a hundred cool
corners, with three tiers of ruffles and a big bow in back until she
shed black and yellow around her in a sort of phosphorescent lustre.
The Jelly-bean's eyes opened wide and a lump arose in his throat. For
she stood beside the door until her partner hurried up. Jim recognized
him as the stranger who had been with her in Joe Ewing's car that
afternoon. He saw her set her arms akimbo and say something in a low
voice, and laugh. The man laughed too and Jim experienced the quick
pang of a weird new kind of pain. Some ray had passed between the
pair, a shaft of beauty from that sun that had warmed him a moment
since. The Jelly-bean felt suddenly like a weed in a shadow.

A minute later Clark approached him, bright-eyed and glowing.

"Hi, old man" he cried with some lack of originality. "How you making
out?"

Jim replied that he was making out as well as could be expected.

"You come along with me," commanded Clark. "I've got something that'll
put an edge on the evening."

Jim followed him awkwardly across the floor and up the stairs to the
locker-room where Clark produced a flask of nameless yellow liquid.

"Good old corn."

Ginger ale arrived on a tray. Such potent nectar as "good old corn"
needed some disguise beyond seltzer.

"Say, boy," exclaimed Clark breathlessly, "doesn't Nancy Lamar look
beautiful?"

Jim nodded.

"Mighty beautiful," he agreed.

"She's all dolled up to a fare-you-well to-night," continued Clark.
"Notice that fellow she's with?"

"Big fella? White pants?"

"Yeah. Well, that's Ogden Merritt from Savannah.
Old man Merritt makes
the Merritt safety razors. This fella's crazy about her.
Been chasing,
after her all year.

"She's a wild baby," continued Clark, "but I like her.
So does
everybody. But she sure does do crazy stunts. She usually gets out
alive, but she's got scars all over her reputation from one thing or

another she's done."

"That so?" Jim passed over his glass. "That's good corn."

"Not so bad. Oh, she's a wild one. Shoot craps, say, boy! And she do
like her high-balls. Promised I'd give her one later on."

"She in love with this--Merritt?"

"Damned if I know. Seems like all the best girls around here marry
fellas and go off somewhere."

He poured himself one more drink and carefully corked the bottle.

"Listen, Jim, I got to go dance and I'd be much obliged if you just
stick this corn right on your hip as long as you're not dancing. If a
man notices I've had a drink he'll come up and ask me and before I

know it it's all gone and somebody else is having my good time."

So Nancy Lamar was going to marry. This toast of a town was to become
the private property of an individual in white trousers--and all
because white trousers' father had made a better razor than his
neighbor. As they descended the stairs Jim found the idea inexplicably
depressing. For the first time in his life he felt a vague and
romantic yearning. A picture of her began to form in his
imagination--Nancy walking boylike and debonnaire along the street,
taking an orange as tithe from a worshipful fruit-dealer, charging a
dope on a mythical account, at Soda Sam's, assembling a convoy of
beaux and then driving off in triumphal state for an afternoon of
splashing and singing.

The Jelly-bean walked out on the porch to a deserted corner, dark

between the moon on the lawn and the single lighted door of the

ballroom. There he found a chair and, lighting a cigarette, drifted

into the thoughtless reverie that was his usual mood. Yet now it was a

reverie made sensuous by the night and by the hot smell of damp powder

puffs, tucked in the fronts of low dresses and distilling a thousand

rich scents, to float out through the open door. The music itself,

blurred by a loud trombone, became hot and shadowy, a languorous

overtone to the scraping of many shoes and slippers.

Suddenly the square of yellow light that fell through the door was

obscured by a dark figure. A girl had come out of the dressing-room

and was standing on the porch not more than ten feet away. Jim heard a

low-breathed "doggone" and then she turned and saw him. It was Nancy

Lamar.

Jim rose to his feet.

"Howdy?"

"Hello--" she paused, hesitated and then approached.
"Oh, it's--Jim
Powell."

He bowed slightly, tried to think of a casual remark.

"Do you suppose," she began quickly, "I mean--do
you know anything
about gum?"

"What?" "I've got gum on my shoe. Some utter ass
left his or her gum
on the floor and of course I stepped in it."

Jim blushed, inappropriately.

"Do you know how to get it off?" she demanded
petulantly. "I've tried
a knife. I've tried every damn thing in the dressing-
room. I've tried

soap and water--and even perfume and I've ruined my powder-puff trying
to make it stick to that."

Jim considered the question in some agitation.

"Why--I think maybe gasolene--"

The words had scarcely left his lips when she grasped his hand and
pulled him at a run off the low veranda, over a flower bed and at a
gallop toward a group of cars parked in the moonlight by the first
hole of the golf course.

"Turn on the gasolene," she commanded breathlessly.

"What?"

"For the gum of course. I've got to get it off. I can't dance with gum
on."

Obediently Jim turned to the cars and began inspecting them with a

view to obtaining the desired solvent. Had she demanded a cylinder he
would have done his best to wrench one out.

"Here," he said after a moment's search. "'Here's one that's easy. Got
a handkerchief?"

"It's up-stairs wet. I used it for the soap and water."

Jim laboriously explored his pockets.

"Don't believe I got one either."

"Doggone it! Well, we can turn it on and let it run on the ground."

He turned the spout; a dripping began.

"More!"

He turned it on fuller. The dripping became a flow and formed an oily
pool that glistened brightly, reflecting a dozen tremulous moons on
its quivering bosom.

"Ah," she sighed contentedly, "let it all out. The only thing to do is
to wade in it."

In desperation he turned on the tap full and the pool suddenly widened
sending tiny rivers and trickles in all directions.

"That's fine. That's something like."

Raising her skirts she stepped gracefully in.

"I know this'll take it off," she murmured.

Jim smiled.

"There's lots more cars."

She stepped daintily out of the gasolene and began scraping her
slippers, side and bottom, on the running-board of the automobile. The
jelly-bean contained himself no longer. He bent double with explosive
laughter and after a second she joined in.

"You're here with Clark Darrow, aren't you?" she asked as they walked
back toward the veranda.

"Yes."

"You know where he is now?"

"Out dancin', I reckin."

"The deuce. He promised me a highball."

"Well," said Jim, "I guess that'll be all right. I got his bottle right
here in my pocket."

She smiled at him radiantly.

"I guess maybe you'll need ginger ale though," he added.

"Not me. Just the bottle."

"Sure enough?"

She laughed scornfully.

"Try me. I can drink anything any man can. Let's sit down."

She perched herself on the side of a table and he dropped into one of
the wicker chairs beside her. Taking out the cork she held the flask
to her lips and took a long drink. He watched her fascinated.

"Like it?"

She shook her head breathlessly.

"No, but I like the way it makes me feel. I think most people are that
way."

Jim agreed.

"My daddy liked it too well. It got him."

"American men," said Nancy gravely, "don't know how to drink."

"What?" Jim was startled.

"In fact," she went on carelessly, "they don't know how to do anything
very well. The one thing I regret in my life is that I wasn't born in
England."

"In England?"

"Yes. It's the one regret of my life that I wasn't."

"Do you like it over there?" "Yes. Immensely. I've never been there in
person, but I've met a lot of Englishmen who were over here in the
army, Oxford and Cambridge men--you know, that's like Sewanee and
University of Georgia are here--and of course I've read a lot of
English novels."

Jim was interested, amazed.

"D' you ever hear of Lady Diana Manner?" she asked earnestly.

No, Jim had not.

"Well, she's what I'd like to be. Dark, you know, like me, and wild as
sin. She's the girl who rode her horse up the steps of some cathedral
or church or something and all the novelists made their heroines do it
afterwards."

Jim nodded politely. He was out of his depths.

"Pass the bottle," suggested Nancy. "I'm going to take another little
one. A little drink wouldn't hurt a baby.

"You see," she continued, again breathless after a draught. "People
over there have style, Nobody has style here. I mean the boys here
aren't really worth dressing up for or doing sensational things for.
Don't you know?"

"I suppose so--I mean I suppose not," murmured Jim.

"And I'd like to do 'em an' all. I'm really the only girl in town that
has style."

She stretched, out her arms and yawned pleasantly.

"Pretty evening."

"Sure is," agreed Jim.

"Like to have boat" she suggested dreamily. "Like to sail out on a
silver lake, say the Thames, for instance. Have champagne and caviare
sandwiches along. Have about eight people. And one of the men would
jump overboard to amuse the party, and get drowned like a man did with
Lady Diana Manners once."

"Did he do it to please her?"

"Didn't mean drown himself to please

her. He just meant to jump overboard and make
everybody laugh."

"I reckin they just died laughin' when he drowned."

"Oh, I suppose they laughed a little," she admitted. "I
imagine she
did, anyway. She's pretty hard, I guess--like I am."

"You hard?"

"Like nails." She yawned again and added, "Give me
a little more from
that bottle."

Jim hesitated but she held out her hand defiantly,
"Don't treat me
like a girl;" she warned him. "I'm not like any girl
you ever
saw," She considered. "Still, perhaps you're right.
You got--you got
old head on young shoulders."

She jumped to her feet and moved toward the door.
The Jelly-bean rose
also.

"Good-bye," she said politely, "good-bye. Thanks, Jelly-bean."

Then she stepped inside and left him wide-eyed upon the porch.

III

At twelve o'clock a procession of cloaks issued single file from the
women's dressing-room and, each one pairing with a coated beau like
dancers meeting in a cotillion figure, drifted through the door with
sleepy happy laughter--through the door into the dark where autos
backed and snorted and parties called to one another and gathered
around the water-cooler.

Jim, sitting in his corner, rose to look for Clark. They had met at

eleven; then Clark had gone in to dance. So, seeking him, Jim wandered
into the soft-drink stand that had once been a bar. The room was
deserted except for a sleepy negro dozing behind the counter and two
boys lazily fingering a pair of dice at one of the tables. Jim was
about to leave when he saw Clark coming in. At the same moment Clark
looked up.

"Hi, Jim" he commanded. "C'mon over and help us with this bottle. I
guess there's not much left, but there's one all around."

Nancy, the man from Savannah, Marylyn Wade, and Joe Ewing were lolling
and laughing in the doorway. Nancy caught Jim's eye and winked at him
humorously.

They drifted over to a table and arranging themselves around it waited

for the waiter to bring ginger ale. Jim, faintly ill at ease, turned
his eyes on Nancy, who had drifted into a nickel crap game with the
two boys at the next table.

"Bring them over here," suggested Clark.

Joe looked around.

"We don't want to draw a crowd. It's against club rules."

"Nobody's around," insisted Clark, "except Mr. Taylor. He's walking up
and down, like a wild-man trying find out who let all the gasolene out
of his car."

There was a general laugh.

"I bet a million Nancy got something on her shoe again. You can't park
when she's around."

"O Nancy, Mr. Taylor's looking for you!"

Nancy's cheeks were glowing with excitement over the game. "I haven't
seen his silly little flivver in two weeks."

Jim felt a sudden silence. He turned and saw an individual of
uncertain age standing in the doorway.

Clark's voice punctuated the embarrassment.

"Won't you join us Mr. Taylor?"

"Thanks."

Mr. Taylor spread his unwelcome presence over a chair. "Have to, I
guess. I'm waiting till they dig me up some gasolene. Somebody got
funny with my car."

His eyes narrowed and he looked quickly from one to the other. Jim
wondered what he had heard from the doorway--tried to remember what
had been said.

"I'm right to-night," Nancy sang out, "and my four bits is in the
ring."

"Faded!" snapped Taylor suddenly.

"Why, Mr. Taylor, I didn't know you shot craps!" Nancy was overjoyed
to find that he had seated himself and instantly covered her bet. They
had openly disliked each other since the night she had definitely
discouraged a series of rather pointed advances.

"All right, babies, do it for your mamma. Just one little seven."
Nancy was _cooing_ to the dice. She rattled them with a brave
underhand flourish, and rolled them out on the table.

"Ah-h! I suspected it. And now again with the dollar up."

Five passes to her credit found Taylor a bad loser. She was making it

personal, and after each success Jim watched triumph flutter across
her face. She was doubling with each throw--such luck could scarcely
last. "Better go easy," he cautioned her timidly.

"Ah, but watch this one," she whispered. It was eight on the dice and
she called her number.

"Little Ada, this time we're going South."

Ada from Decatur rolled over the table. Nancy was flushed and
half-hysterical, but her luck was holding.

She drove the pot up and up, refusing to drag. Taylor was drumming
with his fingers on the table but he was in to stay.

Then Nancy tried for a ten and lost the dice. Taylor seized them
avidly. He shot in silence, and in the hush of excitement the clatter
of one pass after another on the table was the only sound.

Now Nancy had the dice again, but her luck had broken. An hour passed.
Back and forth it went. Taylor had been at it again-- and again and
again. They were even at last--Nancy lost her ultimate five dollars.

"Will you take my check," she said quickly, "for fifty, and we'll
shoot it all?" Her voice was a little unsteady and her hand shook as
she reached to the money.

Clark exchanged an uncertain but alarmed glance with Joe Ewing. Taylor
shot again. He had Nancy's check.

"How 'bout another?" she said wildly. "Jes' any bank'll do--money
everywhere as a matter of fact."

Jim understood--the "good old corn" he had given her--the "good old
corn" she had taken since. He wished he dared interfere--a girl of

that age and position would hardly have two bank accounts. When the
clock struck two he contained himself no longer.

"May I--can't you let me roll 'em for you?" he suggested, his low,
lazy voice a little strained.

Suddenly sleepy and listless, Nancy flung the dice down before him.

"All right--old boy! As Lady Diana Manners says, 'Shoot 'em,
Jelly-bean'--My luck's gone."

"Mr. Taylor," said Jim, carelessly, "we'll shoot for one of those
there checks against the cash."

Half an hour later Nancy swayed forward and clapped him on the back.

"Stole my luck, you did." She was nodding her head sagely.

Jim swept up the last check and putting it with the others tore them
into confetti and scattered them on the floor. Someone started singing
and Nancy kicking her chair backward rose to her feet.

"Ladies and gentlemen," she announced, "Ladies-- that's you Marylyn. I
want to tell the world that Mr. Jim Powell, who is a well-known
Jelly-bean of this city, is an exception to the great rule--'lucky in
dice--unlucky in love.' He's lucky in dice, and as matter of fact I--I
love him. Ladies and gentlemen, Nancy Lamar, famous dark-haired
beauty often featured in the _Herald_ as one the most popular
members of younger set as other girls are often featured in this
particular case; Wish to announce--wish to announce, anyway,
Gentlemen--" She tipped suddenly. Clark caught her and restored her
balance.

"My error," she laughed, "she--stoops to--stoops to--anyways--We'll
drink to Jelly-bean ... Mr. Jim Powell, King of the Jelly-beans."

And a few minutes later as Jim waited hat in hand for Clark in the
darkness of that same corner of the porch where she had come searching
for gasolene, she appeared suddenly beside him.

"Jelly-bean," she said, "are you here, Jelly-bean? I think--" and her
slight unsteadiness seemed part of an enchanted dream--"I think you
deserve one of my sweetest kisses for that, Jelly-bean."

For an instant her arms were around his neck--her lips were pressed to
his.

"I'm a wild part of the world, Jelly-bean, but you did me a good
turn."

Then she was gone, down the porch, over the cricket-loud lawn. Jim saw

Merritt come out the front door and say something to her angrily--saw

her laugh and, turning away, walk with averted eyes to his car.

Marylyn and Joe followed, singing a drowsy song about a Jazz baby.

Clark came out and joined Jim on the steps. "All pretty lit, I guess,"

he yawned. "Merritt's in a mean mood. He's certainly off Nancy."

Over east along the golf course a faint rug of gray spread itself

across the feet of the night. The party in the car began to chant a

chorus as the engine warmed up.

"Good-night everybody," called Clark.

"Good-night, Clark."

"Good-night."

There was a pause, and then a soft, happy voice added,

"Good-night, Jelly-bean."

The car drove off to a burst of singing. A rooster on a farm across
the way took up a solitary mournful crow, and behind them, a last
negro waiter turned out the porch light, Jim and Clark strolled over
toward the Ford, their shoes crunching raucously on the gravel drive.

"Oh boy!" sighed Clark softly, "how you can set those dice!"

It was still too dark for him to see the flush on Jim's thin
cheeks--or to know that it was a flush of unfamiliar shame.

IV

Over Tilly's garage a bleak room echoed all day to the rumble and
snorting down-stairs and the singing of the negro washers as they
turned the hose on the cars outside. It was a cheerless square of a
room, punctuated with a bed and a battered table on which lay half a
dozen books--Joe Miller's "Slow Train thru Arkansas," "Lucille," in an
old edition very much annotated in an old-fashioned hand; "The Eyes of
the World," by Harold Bell Wright, and an ancient prayer-book of the
Church of England with the name Alice Powell and the date 1831 written
on the fly-leaf.

The East, gray when Jelly-bean entered the garage, became a rich and
vivid blue as he turned on his solitary electric light. He snapped it
out again, and going to the window rested his elbows on the sill and

stared into the deepening morning. With the awakening of his emotions,
his first perception was a sense of futility, a dull ache at the utter
grayness of his life. A wall had sprung up suddenly around him hedging
him in, a wall as definite and tangible as the white wall of his bare
room. And with his perception of this wall all that had been the
romance of his existence, the casualness, the light-hearted
improvidence, the miraculous open-handedness of life faded out. The
Jelly-bean strolling up Jackson Street humming a lazy song, known at
every shop and street stand, cropful of easy greeting and local wit,
sad sometimes for only the sake of sadness and the flight of
time--that Jelly-bean was suddenly vanished. The very name was a
reproach, a triviality. With a flood of insight he knew that Merritt
must despise him, that even Nancy's kiss in the dawn would have

awakened not jealousy but only a contempt for Nancy's so lowering
herself. And on his part the Jelly-bean had used for her a dingy
subterfuge learned from the garage. He had been her moral laundry; the
stains were his.

As the gray became blue, brightened and filled the room, he crossed to
his bed and threw himself down on it, gripping the edges fiercely.

"I love her," he cried aloud, "God!"

As he said this something gave way within him like a lump melting in
his throat. The air cleared and became radiant with dawn, and turning
over on his face he began to sob dully into the pillow.

In the sunshine of three o'clock Clark Darrow chugging painfully along
Jackson Street was hailed by the Jelly-bean, who stood on the curb
with his fingers in his vest pockets.

"Hi!" called Clark, bringing his Ford to an astonishing stop
alongside. "Just get up?"

The Jelly-bean shook his head.

"Never did go to bed. Felt sorta restless, so I took a long walk this
morning out in the country. Just got into town this minute."

"Should think you _would_ feel restless. I been feeling thataway
all day--"

"I'm thinkin' of leavin' town" continued the Jelly-bean, absorbed by
his own thoughts. "Been thinkin' of goin' up on the farm, and takin' a
little that work off Uncle Dun. Reckin I been bummin' too long."

Clark was silent and the Jelly-bean continued:

"I reckin maybe after Aunt Mamie dies I could sink that money of mine
in the farm and make somethin' out of it. All my people originally
came from that part up there. Had a big place."

Clark looked at him curiously.

"That's funny," he said. "This--this sort of affected me the same
way."

The Jelly-bean hesitated.

"I don't know," he began slowly, "somethin' about--about that girl
last night talkin' about a lady named Diana Manners--an English lady,
sorta got me thinkin'!" He drew himself up and looked oddly at Clark,
"I had a family once," he said defiantly.

Clark nodded.

"I know."

"And I'm the last of 'em," continued the Jelly-bean his voice rising
slightly, "and I ain't worth shucks. Name they call me by means
jelly--weak and wobbly like. People who weren't nothin' when my folks
was a lot turn up their noses when they pass me on the street."

Again Clark was silent.

"So I'm through, I'm goin' to-day. And when I come back to this town
it's going to be like a gentleman."

Clark took out his handkerchief and wiped his damp brow.

"Reckon you're not the only one it shook up," he admitted gloomily.
"All this thing of girls going round like they do is going to stop
right quick. Too bad, too, but everybody'll have to see it thataway."

"Do you mean," demanded Jim in surprise, "that all that's leaked out?"

"Leaked out? How on earth could they keep it secret. It'll be
announced in the papers to-night. Doctor Lamar's got to save his name
somehow."

Jim put his hands on the sides of the car and tightened his long
fingers on the metal.

"Do you mean Taylor investigated those checks?"

It was Clark's turn to be surprised.

"Haven't you heard what happened?"

Jim's startled eyes were answer enough.

"Why," announced Clark dramatically, "those four got another bottle of
corn, got tight and decided to shock the town--so Nancy and that fella

Merritt were married in Rockville at seven o'clock this morning."

A tiny indentation appeared in the metal under the Jelly-bean's
fingers.

"Married?"

"Sure enough. Nancy sobered up and rushed back into town, crying and
frightened to death--claimed it'd all been a mistake. First Doctor
Lamar went wild and was going to kill Merritt, but finally they got it
patched up some way, and Nancy and Merritt went to Savannah on the
two-thirty train."

Jim closed his eyes and with an effort overcame a sudden sickness.

"It's too bad," said Clark philosophically. "I don't mean the
wedding--reckon that's all right, though I don't guess Nancy cared a

darn about him. But it's a crime for a nice girl like that to hurt her
family that way."

The Jelly-bean let go the car and turned away. Again something was
going on inside him, some inexplicable but almost chemical change.

"Where you going?" asked Clark.

The Jelly-bean turned and looked dully back over his shoulder.

"Got to go," he muttered. "Been up too long; feelin' right sick."

"Oh."

*   *   *   *   *

The street was hot at three and hotter still at four, the April dust
seeming to enmesh the sun and give it forth again as a world-old joke

forever played on an eternity of afternoons. But at half past four a

first layer of quiet fell and the shades lengthened under the awnings

and heavy foliaged trees. In this heat nothing mattered. All life was

weather, a waiting through the hot where events had no significance

for the cool that was soft and caressing like a woman's hand on a

tired forehead. Down in Georgia there is a feeling--perhaps

inarticulate--that this is the greatest wisdom of the South--so after

a while the Jelly-bean turned into a poolhall on Jackson Street where

he was sure to find a congenial crowd who would make all the old

jokes--the ones he knew.

THE CAMEL'S BACK

The glazed eye of the tired reader resting for a second on the above

title will presume it to be merely metaphorical. Stories about the cup

and the lip and the bad penny and the new broom rarely have anything,

to do with cups or lips or pennies or brooms. This story Is the

exception. It has to do with a material, visible and large-as-life

camel's back.

Starting from the neck we shall work toward the tail. I want you to

meet Mr. Perry Parkhurst, twenty-eight, lawyer, native of Toledo.

Perry has nice teeth, a Harvard diploma, parts his hair in the middle.

You have met him before--in Cleveland, Portland, St. Paul,

Indianapolis, Kansas City, and so forth. Baker Brothers, New York,

pause on their semi-annual trip through the West to clothe him;

Montmorency & Co. dispatch a young man post-haste every three months

to see that he has the correct number of little punctures on his
shoes. He has a domestic roadster now, will have a French roadster if
he lives long enough, and doubtless a Chinese tank if it comes into
fashion. He looks like the advertisement of the young man rubbing his
sunset-colored chest with liniment and goes East every other year to
his class reunion.

I want you to meet his Love. Her name is Betty Medill, and she would
take well in the movies. Her father gives her three hundred a month to
dress on, and she has tawny eyes and hair and feather fans of five
colors. I shall also introduce her father, Cyrus Medill. Though he is
to all appearances flesh and blood, he is, strange to say, commonly
known in Toledo as the Aluminum Man. But when he sits in his club
window with two or three Iron Men, and the White Pine Man, and the

Brass Man, they look very much as you and I do, only more so, if you
know what I mean.

Now during the Christmas holidays of 1919 there took place in Toledo,
counting only the people with the italicized _the_, forty-one
dinner parties, sixteen dances, six luncheons, male and female, twelve
teas, four stag dinners, two weddings, and thirteen bridge parties. It
was the cumulative effect of all this that moved Perry Parkhurst on
the twenty-ninth day of December to a decision.

This Medill girl would marry him and she wouldn't marry him. She was
having such a good time that she hated to take such a definite step.
Meanwhile, their secret engagement had got so long that it seemed as
if any day it might break off of its own weight. A little man named
Warburton, who knew it all, persuaded Perry to superman her, to get a

marriage license and go up to the Medill house and tell her she'd have

to marry him at once or call it off forever. So he presented himself,

his heart, his license, and his ultimatum, and within five minutes

they were in the midst of a violent quarrel, a burst of sporadic open

fighting such as occurs near the end of all long wars and engagements.

It brought about one of those ghastly lapses in which two people who

are in love pull up sharp, look at each other coolly and think it's

all been a mistake. Afterward they usually kiss wholesomely and assure

the other person it was all their fault. Say it all was my fault! Say

it was! I want to hear you say it!

But while reconciliation was trembling in the air, while each was, in

a measure, stalling it off, so that they might the more voluptuously

and sentimentally enjoy it when it came, they were permanently interrupted by a twenty-minute phone call for Betty from a garrulous

aunt. At the end of eighteen minutes Perry Parkhurst, urged on by

pride and suspicion and injured dignity, put on his long fur coat,

picked up his light brown soft hat, and stalked out the door.

"It's all over," he muttered brokenly as he tried to jam his car into

first. "It's all over--if I have to choke you for an hour, damn you!".

The last to the car, which had been standing some time and was quite

cold.

He drove downtown--that is, he got into a snow rut that led him

downtown. He sat slouched down very low in his seat, much too

dispirited to care where he went.

In front of the Clarendon Hotel he was hailed from the sidewalk by a

bad man named Baily, who had big teeth and lived at the hotel and had
never been in love.

"Perry," said the bad man softly when the roadster drew up beside him
at the curb, "I've got six quarts of the doggonedest still champagne
you ever tasted. A third of it's yours, Perry, if you'll come
up-stairs and help Martin Macy and me drink it."

"Baily," said Perry tensely, "I'll drink your champagne. I'll drink
every drop of it, I don't care if it kills me."

"Shut up, you nut!" said the bad man gently. "They don't put wood
alcohol in champagne. This is the stuff that proves the world is more
than six thousand years old. It's so ancient that the cork is
petrified. You have to pull it with a stone drill."

"Take me up-stairs," said Perry moodily. "If that cork sees my heart it'll fall out from pure mortification."

The room up-stairs was full of those innocent hotel pictures of little
girls eating apples and sitting in swings and talking to dogs. The
other decorations were neckties and a pink man reading a pink paper
devoted to ladies in pink tights.

"When you have to go into the highways and byways----" said the pink
man, looking reproachfully at Baily and Perry.

"Hello, Martin Macy," said Perry shortly, "where's this stone-age
champagne?"

"What's the rush? This isn't an operation, understand. This is a
party."

Perry sat down dully and looked disapprovingly at all the neckties.

Baily leisurely opened the door of a wardrobe and brought out six
handsome bottles.

"Take off that darn fur coat!" said Martin Macy to Perry. "Or maybe
you'd like to have us open all the windows."

"Give me champagne," said Perry.

"Going to the Townsends' circus ball to-night?"

"Am not!"

"'Vited?"

"Uh-huh."

"Why not go?"

"Oh, I'm sick of parties," exclaimed Perry. "I'm sick of 'em. I've
been to so many that I'm sick of 'em."

"Maybe you're going to the Howard Tates' party?"

"No, I tell you; I'm sick of 'em."

"Well," said Macy consolingly, "the Tates' is just for college kids
anyways."

"I tell you----"

"I thought you'd be going to one of 'em anyways. I see by the papers
you haven't missed a one this Christmas."

"Hm," grunted Perry morosely.

He would never go to any more parties. Classical phrases played in his
mind--that side of his life was closed, closed. Now when a man says
"closed, closed" like that, you can be pretty sure that some woman has
double-closed him, so to speak. Perry was also thinking that other
classical thought, about how cowardly suicide is. A noble thought that
one--warm and inspiring. Think of all the fine men we should lose if

suicide were not so cowardly!

An hour later was six o'clock, and Perry had lost all resemblance to
the young man in the liniment advertisement. He looked like a rough
draft for a riotous cartoon. They were singing--an impromptu song of
Baily's improvisation:

_"One Lump Perry, the parlor snake,
Famous through the city for the way he drinks his tea;
Plays with it, toys with it
Makes no noise with it,
Balanced on a napkin on his well-trained knee--"_

"Trouble is," said Perry, who had just banged his hair with Baily's
comb and was tying an orange tie round it to get the effect of Julius
Caesar, "that you fellas can't sing worth a damn. Soon's I leave the
air and start singing tenor you start singin' tenor too."

"'M a natural tenor," said Macy gravely. "Voice lacks cultivation,
tha's all. Gotta natural voice, m'aunt used say. Naturally good
singer."

"Singers, singers, all good singers," remarked Baily, who was at the
telephone. "No, not the cabaret; I want night egg. I mean some
dog-gone clerk 'at's got food--food! I want----"

"Julius Caesar," announced Perry, turning round from the mirror. "Man
of iron will and stern 'termination."

"Shut up!" yelled Baily. "Say, iss Mr. Baily Sen' up enormous supper.
Use y'own judgment. Right away."

He connected the receiver and the hook with some difficulty, and then
with his lips closed and an expression of solemn intensity in his eyes
went to the lower drawer of his dresser and pulled it open.

"Lookit!" he commanded. In his hands he held a truncated garment of
pink gingham.

"Pants," he exclaimed gravely. "Lookit!"

This was a pink blouse, a red tie, and a Buster Brown collar.

"Lookit!" he repeated. "Costume for the Townsends' circus ball. I'm
li'l' boy carries water for the elephants."

Perry was impressed in spite of himself.

"I'm going to be Julius Caesar," he announced after a moment of
concentration.

"Thought you weren't going!" said Macy.

"Me? Sure I'm goin', Never miss a party. Good for the nerves--like
celery."

"Caesar!" scoffed Baily. "Can't be Caesar! He is not about a circus.
Caesar's Shakespeare. Go as a clown."

Perry shook his head.

"Nope; Caesar,"

"Caesar?"

"Sure. Chariot."

Light dawned on Baily.

"That's right. Good idea."

Perry looked round the room searchingly.

"You lend me a bathrobe and this tie," he said finally.
Baily
considered.

"No good."

"Sure, tha's all I need. Caesar was a savage. They can't kick if I come as Caesar, if he was a savage."

"No," said Baily, shaking his head slowly. "Get a costume over at a
costumer's. Over at Nolak's."

"Closed up."

"Find out."

After a puzzling five minutes at the phone a small, weary voice
managed to convince Perry that it was Mr. Nolak speaking, and that
they would remain open until eight because of the Townsends' ball.
Thus assured, Perry ate a great amount of filet mignon and drank his
third of the last bottle of champagne. At eight-fifteen the man in the
tall hat who stands in front of the Clarendon found him trying to
start his roadster.

"Froze up," said Perry wisely. "The cold froze it. The cold air."

"Froze, eh?"

"Yes. Cold air froze it."

"Can't start it?"

"Nope. Let it stand here till summer. One those hot ole August days'll
thaw it out awright."

"Goin' let it stand?"

"Sure. Let 'er stand. Take a hot thief to steal it. Gemme taxi."

The man in the tall hat summoned a taxi.

"Where to, mister?"

"Go to Nolak's--costume fella."

II

Mrs. Nolak was short and ineffectual looking, and on the cessation of
the world war had belonged for a while to one of the new
nationalities. Owing to unsettled European conditions she had never
since been quite sure what she was. The shop in which she and her
husband performed their daily stint was dim and ghostly, and peopled
with suits of armor and Chinese mandarins, and enormous papier-mâché
birds suspended from the ceiling. In a vague background many rows of
masks glared eyelessly at the visitor, and there were glass cases full
of crowns and scepters, and jewels and enormous stomachers, and
paints, and crape hair, and wigs of all colors.

When Perry ambled into the shop Mrs. Nolak was folding up the last
troubles of a strenuous day, so she thought, in a drawer full of pink
silk stockings.

"Something for you?" she queried pessimistically.
"Want costume of
Julius Hur, the charioteer."

Mrs. Nolak was sorry, but every stitch of charioteer
had been rented
long ago. Was it for the Townsends' circus ball?

It was.

"Sorry," she said, "but I don't think there's anything
left that's
really circus."

This was an obstacle.

"Hm," said Perry. An idea struck him suddenly. "If
you've got a piece
of canvas I could go's a tent."

"Sorry, but we haven't anything like that. A hardware
store is where
you'd have to go to. We have some very nice
Confederate soldiers."

"No. No soldiers."

"And I have a very handsome king."

He shook his head.

"Several of the gentlemen" she continued hopefully,
"are wearing
stovepipe hats and swallow-tail coats and going as
ringmasters--but
we're all out of tall hats. I can let you have some
crape hair for a
mustache."

"Want somep'n 'stinctive."

"Something--let's see. Well, we have a lion's head,
and a goose, and a
camel--"

"Camel?" The idea seized Perry's imagination,
gripped it fiercely.

"Yes, but It needs two people."

"Camel, That's the idea. Lemme see it."

The camel was produced from his resting place on a top shelf. At first
glance he appeared to consist entirely of a very gaunt, cadaverous
head and a sizable hump, but on being spread out he was found to
possess a dark brown, unwholesome-looking body made of thick, cottony
cloth.

"You see it takes two people," explained Mrs. Nolak, holding the camel
in frank admiration. "If you have a friend he could be part of it. You
see there's sorta pants for two people. One pair is for the fella in
front, and the other pair for the fella in back. The fella in front
does the lookin' out through these here eyes, an' the fella in back
he's just gotta stoop over an' folla the front fella round."

"Put it on," commanded Perry.

Obediently Mrs. Nolak put her tabby-cat face inside
the camel's head
and turned it from side to side ferociously.

Perry was fascinated.

"What noise does a camel make?"

"What?" asked Mrs. Nolak as her face emerged,
somewhat smudgy. "Oh,
what noise? Why, he sorta brays."

"Lemme see it in a mirror."

Before a wide mirror Perry tried on the head and
turned from side to
side appraisingly. In the dim light the effect was
distinctly
pleasing. The camel's face was a study in pessimism,
decorated with
numerous abrasions, and it must be admitted that his
coat was in that
state of general negligence peculiar to camels--in
fact, he needed to
be cleaned and pressed--but distinctive he certainly
was. He was

majestic. He would have attracted attention in any gathering, if only
by his melancholy cast of feature and the look of hunger lurking round
his shadowy eyes.

"You see you have to have two people," said Mrs. Nolak again.

Perry tentatively gathered up the body and legs and wrapped them about
him, tying the hind legs as a girdle round his waist. The effect on
the whole was bad. It was even irreverent--like one of those mediaeval
pictures of a monk changed into a beast by the ministrations of Satan.
At the very best the ensemble resembled a humpbacked cow sitting on
her haunches among blankets.

"Don't look like anything at all," objected Perry gloomily.

"No," said Mrs. Nolak; "you see you got to have two people."

A solution flashed upon Perry.

"You got a date to-night?"

"Oh, I couldn't possibly----"

"Oh, come on," said Perry encouragingly. "Sure you can! Here! Be good
sport, and climb into these hind legs."

With difficulty he located them, and extended their yawning depths
ingratiatingly. But Mrs. Nolak seemed loath. She backed perversely
away.

"Oh, no----"

"C'mon! You can be the front if you want to. Or we'll flip a coin."

"Make it worth your while."

Mrs. Nolak set her lips firmly together.

"Now you just stop!" she said with no coyness implied. "None of the
gentlemen ever acted up this way before. My husband----"

"You got a husband?" demanded Perry. "Where is he?"

"He's home."

"Wha's telephone number?"

After considerable parley he obtained the telephone number pertaining
to the Nolak penates and got into communication with that small, weary
voice he had heard once before that day. But Mr. Nolak, though taken
off his guard and somewhat confused by Perry's brilliant flow of
logic, stuck staunchly to his point. He refused firmly, but with
dignity, to help out Mr. Parkhurst in the capacity of back part of a
camel.

Having rung off, or rather having been rung off on, Perry sat down on
a three-legged stool to think it over. He named over to himself those
friends on whom he might call, and then his mind paused as Betty
Medill's name hazily and sorrowfully occurred to him. He had a
sentimental thought. He would ask her. Their love affair was over, but
she could not refuse this last request. Surely it was not much to
ask--to help him keep up his end of social obligation for one short
night. And if she insisted, she could be the front part of the camel
and he would go as the back. His magnanimity pleased him. His mind
even turned to rosy-colored dreams of a tender reconciliation inside
the camel--there hidden away from all the world....

"Now you'd better decide right off."

The bourgeois voice of Mrs. Nolak broke in upon his mellow fancies and roused him to action. He went to the phone and called up the Medill

house. Miss Betty was out; had gone out to dinner.

Then, when all seemed lost, the camel's back wandered curiously into

the store. He was a dilapidated individual with a cold in his head and

a general trend about him of downwardness. His cap was pulled down low

on his head, and his chin was pulled down low on his chest, his coat

hung down to his shoes, he looked run-down, down at the heels,

and--Salvation Army to the contrary--down and out. He said that he was

the taxicab-driver that the gentleman had hired at the Clarendon

Hotel. He had been instructed to wait outside, but he had waited some

time, and a suspicion had grown upon him that the gentleman had gone

out the back way with purpose to defraud him-- gentlemen sometimes

did--so he had come in. He sank down onto the three-legged stool.

"Wanta go to a party?" demanded Perry sternly.

"I gotta work," answered the taxi-driver lugubriously.
"I gotta keep
my job."

"It's a very good party."

"'S a very good job."

"Come on!" urged Perry. "Be a good fella. See--it's
pretty!" He held
the camel up and the taxi-driver looked at it
cynically.

"Huh!"

Perry searched feverishly among the folds of the
cloth.

"See!" he cried enthusiastically, holding up a
selection of folds.
"This is your part. You don't even have to talk. All
you have to do is

to walk--and sit down occasionally. You do all the sitting down. Think
of it. I'm on my feet all the time and _you_ can sit down some of
the time. The only time _I_ can sit down is when we're lying
down, and you can sit down when--oh, any time. See?"

"What's 'at thing?" demanded the individual dubiously. "A shroud?"

"Not at all," said Perry indignantly. "It's a camel."

"Huh?"

Then Perry mentioned a sum of money, and the conversation left the
land of grunts and assumed a practical tinge. Perry and the
taxi-driver tried on the camel in front of the mirror.

"You can't see it," explained Perry, peering anxiously out through the
eyeholes, "but honestly, ole man, you look sim'ly great! Honestly!"

A grunt from the hump acknowledged this somewhat dubious compliment.

"Honestly, you look great!" repeated Perry enthusiastically. "Move
round a little."

The hind legs moved forward, giving the effect of a huge cat-camel
hunching his back preparatory to a spring.

"No; move sideways."

The camel's hips went neatly out of joint; a hula dancer would have
writhed in envy.

"Good, isn't it?" demanded Perry, turning to Mrs. Nolak for approval.

"It looks lovely," agreed Mrs. Nolak.

"We'll take it," said Perry.

The bundle was stowed under Perry's arm and they left the shop.

"Go to the party!" he commanded as he took his seat in the back.

"What party?"

"Fanzy-dress party."

"Where'bouts is it?"

This presented a new problem. Perry tried to remember, but the names
of all those who had given parties during the holidays danced
confusedly before his eyes. He could ask Mrs. Nolak, but on looking
out the window he saw that the shop was dark. Mrs. Nolak had already
faded out, a little black smudge far down the snowy street.

"Drive uptown," directed Perry with fine confidence. "If you see a party, stop. Otherwise I'll tell you when we get there."

He fell into a hazy daydream and his thoughts wandered again to
Betty--he imagined vaguely that they had had a disagreement because
she refused to go to the party as the back part of the camel. He was
just slipping off into a chilly doze when he was wakened by the
taxi-driver opening the door and shaking him by the arm.

"Here we are, maybe."

Perry looked out sleepily. A striped awning led from the curb up to a
spreading gray stone house, from which issued the low drummy whine of
expensive jazz. He recognized the Howard Tate house.

"Sure," he said emphatically; "'at's it! Tate's party to-night. Sure,
everybody's goin'."

"Say," said the individual anxiously after another look at the awning,
"you sure these people ain't gonna romp on me for comin' here?"

Perry drew himself up with dignity.

"'F anybody says anything to you, just tell 'em you're part of my
costume."

The visualization of himself as a thing rather than a person seemed to
reassure the individual.

"All right," he said reluctantly.

Perry stepped out under the shelter of the awning and began unrolling
the camel.

"Let's go," he commanded.

Several minutes later a melancholy, hungry-looking camel, emitting

clouds of smoke from his mouth and from the tip of his noble hump,
might have been seen crossing the threshold of the Howard Tate
residence, passing a startled footman without so much as a snort, and
heading directly for the main stairs that led up to the ballroom. The
beast walked with a peculiar gait which varied between an uncertain
lockstep and a stampede--but can best be described by the word
"halting." The camel had a halting gait--and as he walked he
alternately elongated and contracted like a gigantic concertina.

III

The Howard Tates are, as every one who lives in Toledo knows, the most
formidable people in town. Mrs. Howard Tate was a Chicago Todd before

she became a Toledo Tate, and the family generally affect that
conscious simplicity which has begun to be the earmark of American
aristocracy. The Tates have reached the stage where they talk about
pigs and farms and look at you icy-eyed if you are not amused. They
have begun to prefer retainers rather than friends as dinner guests,
spend a lot of money in a quiet way, and, having lost all sense of
competition, are in process of growing quite dull.

The dance this evening was for little Millicent Tate, and though all
ages were represented, the dancers were mostly from school and
college--the younger married crowd was at the Townsends' circus ball
up at the Tallyho Club. Mrs. Tate was standing just inside tie
ballroom, following Millicent round with her eyes, and beaming
whenever she caught her bye. Beside her were two middle-aged

sycophants, who were saying what a perfectly exquisite child Millicent
was. It was at this moment that Mrs. Tate was grasped firmly by the
skirt and her youngest daughter, Emily, aged eleven, hurled herself
with an "Oof!" into her mother's arms.

"Why, Emily, what's the trouble?"

"Mamma," said Emily, wild-eyed but voluble, "there's something out on
the stairs."

"What?"

"There's a thing out on the stairs, mamma. I think it's a big dog,
mamma, but it doesn't look like a dog."

"What do you mean, Emily?"

The sycophants waved their heads sympathetically.

"Mamma, it looks like a--like a camel."

Mrs. Tate laughed.

"You saw a mean old shadow, dear, that's all."

"No, I didn't. No, it was some kind of thing, mamma-
-big. I was going
down-stairs to see if there were any more people, and
this dog or
something, he was coming up-stairs. Kinda funny,
mamma, like he was
lame. And then he saw me and gave a sort of growl,
and then he slipped
at the top of the landing, and I ran."

Mrs. Tate's laugh faded.

"The child must have seen something," she said.

The sycophants agreed that the child must have seen
something--and
suddenly all three women took an instinctive step
away from the door
as the sounds of muffled steps were audible just
outside.

And then three startled gasps rang out as a dark brown form rounded
the corner, and they saw what was apparently a huge beast looking down
at them hungrily.

"Oof!" cried Mrs. Tate.

"O-o-oh!" cried the ladies in a chorus.

The camel suddenly humped his back, and the gasps turned to shrieks.

"Oh--look!"

"What is it?"

The dancing stopped, bat the dancers hurrying over got quite a
different impression of the invader; in fact, the young people
immediately suspected that it was a stunt, a hired entertainer come to
amuse the party. The boys in long trousers looked at it rather

disdainfully, and sauntered over with their hands in their pockets,
feeling that their intelligence was being insulted. But the girls
uttered little shouts of glee.

"It's a camel!"

"Well, if he isn't the funniest!"

The camel stood there uncertainly, swaying slightly from side to aide,
and seeming to take in the room in a careful, appraising glance; then
as if he had come to an abrupt decision, he turned and ambled swiftly
out the door.

Mr. Howard Tate had just come out of the library on the lower floor,
and was standing chatting with a young man in the hall. Suddenly they
heard the noise of shouting up-stairs, and almost immediately a
succession of bumping sounds, followed by the precipitous appearance

at the foot of the stairway of a large brown beast that seemed to be
going somewhere in a great hurry.

"Now what the devil!" said Mr. Tate, starting.

The beast picked itself up not without dignity and, affecting an air
of extreme nonchalance, as if he had just remembered an important
engagement, started at a mixed gait toward the front door. In fact,
his front legs began casually to run.

"See here now," said Mr. Tate sternly. "Here! Grab it, Butterfield!
Grab it!"

The young man enveloped the rear of the camel in a pair of compelling
arms, and, realizing that further locomotion was impossible, the front
end submitted to capture and stood resignedly in a state of some
agitation. By this time a flood of young people was pouring

down-stairs, and Mr. Tate, suspecting everything from an ingenious
burglar to an escaped lunatic, gave crisp directions to the young man:

"Hold him! Lead him in here; we'll soon see."

The camel consented to be led into the library, and Mr. Tate, after
locking the door, took a revolver from a table drawer and instructed
the young man to take the thing's head off. Then he gasped and
returned the revolver to its hiding-place.

"Well, Perry Parkhurst!" he exclaimed in amazement.

"Got the wrong party, Mr. Tate," said Perry sheepishly. "Hope I didn't
scare you."

"Well--you gave us a thrill, Perry." Realization dawned on him.
"You're bound for the Townsends' circus ball."

"That's the general idea."

"Let me introduce Mr. Butterfield, Mr. Parkhurst."
Then turning to
Perry; "Butterfield is staying with us for a few days."

"I got a little mixed up," mumbled Perry. "I'm very
sorry."

"Perfectly all right; most natural mistake in the world.
I've got a
clown rig and I'm going down there myself after a
while." He turned to
Butterfield. "Better change your mind and come
down with us."

The young man demurred. He was going to bed.

"Have a drink, Perry?" suggested Mr. Tate.

"Thanks, I will."

"And, say," continued Tate quickly, "I'd forgotten all
about
your--friend here." He indicated the rear part of the
camel. "I didn't

mean to seem discourteous. Is it any one I know? Bring him out."

"It's not a friend," explained Perry hurriedly. "I just rented him."

"Does he drink?"

"Do you?" demanded Perry, twisting himself tortuously round.

There was a faint sound of assent.

"Sure he does!" said Mr. Tate heartily. "A really efficient camel
ought to be able to drink enough so it'd last him three days."

"Tell you," said Perry anxiously, "he isn't exactly dressed up enough
to come out. If you give me the bottle I can hand it back to him and
he can take his inside."

From under the cloth was audible the enthusiastic smacking sound

inspired by this suggestion. When a butler had appeared with bottles,
glasses, and siphon one of the bottles was handed back; thereafter the
silent partner could be heard imbibing long potations at frequent
intervals.

Thus passed a benign hour. At ten o'clock Mr. Tate decided that they'd
better be starting. He donned his clown's costume; Perry replaced the
camel's head, arid side by side they traversed on foot the single
block between the Tate house and the Tallyho Club.

The circus ball was in full swing. A great tent fly had been put up
inside the ballroom and round the walls had been built rows of booths
representing the various attractions of a circus side show, but these
were now vacated and over the floor swarmed a shouting, laughing
medley of youth and color--downs, bearded ladies, acrobats, bareback

riders, ringmasters, tattooed men, and charioteers. The Townsends had
determined to assure their party of success, so a great quantity of
liquor had been surreptitiously brought over from their house and was
now flowing freely. A green ribbon ran along the wall completely round
the ballroom, with pointing arrows alongside and signs which
instructed the uninitiated to "Follow the green line!" The green line
led down to the bar, where waited pure punch and wicked punch and
plain dark-green bottles.

On the wall above the bar was another arrow, red and very wavy, and
under it the slogan: "Now follow this!"

But even amid the luxury of costume and high spirits represented,
there, the entrance of the camel created something of a stir, and
Perry was immediately surrounded by a curious, laughing crowd

attempting to penetrate the identity of this beast that stood by the
wide doorway eying the dancers with his hungry, melancholy gaze.

And then Perry saw Betty standing in front of a booth, talking to a
comic policeman. She was dressed in the costume of an Egyptian
snake-charmer: her tawny hair was braided and drawn through brass
rings, the effect crowned with a glittering Oriental tiara. Her fair
face was stained to a warm olive glow and on her arms and the half
moon of her back writhed painted serpents with single eyes of venomous
green. Her feet were in sandals and her skirt was slit to the knees,
so that when she walked one caught a glimpse of other slim serpents
painted just above her bare ankles. Wound about her neck was a
glittering cobra. Altogether a charming costume--one that caused the

more nervous among the older women to shrink away from her when she

passed, and the more troublesome ones to make great talk about

"shouldn't be allowed" and "perfectly disgraceful."

But Perry, peering through the uncertain eyes of the camel, saw only

her face, radiant, animated, and glowing with excitement, and her arms

and shoulders, whose mobile, expressive gestures made her always the

outstanding figure in any group. He was fascinated and his fascination

exercised a sobering effect on him. With a growing clarity the events

of the day came back--rage rose within him, and with a half-formed

intention of taking her away from the crowd he started toward her--or

rather he elongated slightly, for he had neglected to issue the

preparatory command necessary to locomotion.

But at this point fickle Kismet, who for a day had played with him bitterly and sardonically, decided to reward him in full for the

amusement he had afforded her. Kismet turned the tawny eyes of the

snake-charmer to the camel. Kismet led her to lean toward the man

beside her and say, "Who's that? That camel?"

"Darned if I know."

But a little man named Warburton, who knew it all, found it necessary
to hazard an opinion:

"It came in with Mr. Tate. I think part of it's probably Warren
Butterfield, the architect from New York, who's visiting the Tates."

Something stirred in Betty Medill--that age-old interest of the
provincial girl in the visiting man.

"Oh," she said casually after a slight pause.

At the end of the next dance Betty and her partner finished up within
a few feet of the camel. With the informal audacity that was the
key-note of the evening she reached out and gently rubbed the camel's
nose.

"Hello, old camel."

The camel stirred uneasily.

"You 'fraid of me?" said Betty, lifting her eyebrows in reproof.
"Don't be. You see I'm a snake-charmer, but I'm pretty good at camels
too."

The camel bowed very low and some one made the obvious remark about
beauty and the beast.

Mrs. Townsend approached the group.

"Well, Mr. Butterfield," she said helpfully, "I wouldn't have recognised you."

Perry bowed again and smiled gleefully behind his mask.

"And who is this with you?" she inquired.

"Oh," said Perry, his voice muffled by the thick cloth and quite
unrecognizable, "he isn't a fellow, Mrs. Townsend. He's just part of
my costume."

Mrs. Townsend laughed and moved away. Perry turned again to Betty,

"So," he thought, "this is how much she cares! On the very day of our
final rupture she starts a flirtation with another man-- an absolute
stranger."

On an impulse he gave her a soft nudge with his shoulder and waved his
head suggestively toward the hall, making it clear that he desired her

to leave her partner and accompany him.

"By-by, Rus," she called to her partner. "This old camel's got me.
Where we going, Prince of Beasts?"

The noble animal made no rejoinder, but stalked gravely along in the
direction of a secluded nook on the side stairs.

There she seated herself, and the camel, after some seconds of
confusion which included gruff orders and sounds of a heated dispute
going on in his interior, placed himself beside her-- his hind legs
stretching out uncomfortably across two steps.

"Well, old egg," said Betty cheerfully, "how do you like our happy
party?"

The old egg indicated that he liked it by rolling his head
ecstatically and executing a gleeful kick with his hoofs.

"This is the first time that I ever had a tête-à-tête with a man's
valet 'round"--she pointed to the hind legs--"or whatever that is."

"Oh," mumbled Perry, "he's deaf and blind."

"I should think you'd feel rather handicapped--you can't very well
toddle, even if you want to."

The camel hang his head lugubriously.

"I wish you'd say something," continued Betty sweetly. "Say you like
me, camel. Say you think I'm beautiful. Say you'd like to belong to a
pretty snake-charmer."

The camel would.

"Will you dance with me, camel?"

The camel would try.

Betty devoted half an hour to the camel. She devoted at least half an
hour to all visiting men. It was usually sufficient. When she
approached a new man the current débutantes were accustomed to scatter
right and left like a close column deploying before a machine-gun. And
so to Perry Parkhurst was awarded the unique privilege of seeing his
love as others saw her. He was flirted with violently!

IV

This paradise of frail foundation was broken into by the sounds of a
general ingress to the ballroom; the cotillion was beginning. Betty
and the camel joined the crowd, her brown hand resting lightly on his
shoulder, defiantly symbolizing her complete adoption of him.

When they entered the couples were already seating themselves at

tables round the walls, and Mrs. Townsend,
resplendent as a super
bareback rider with rather too rotund calves, was
standing in the
centre with the ringmaster in charge of arrangements.
At a signal to
the band every one rose and began to dance.

"Isn't it just slick!" sighed Betty. "Do you think you
can possibly
dance?"

Perry nodded enthusiastically. He felt suddenly
exuberant. After all,
he was here incognito talking to his love--he could
wink
patronizingly at the world.

So Perry danced the cotillion. I say danced, but that is
stretching
the word far beyond the wildest dreams of the
jazziest terpsichorean.
He suffered his partner to put her hands on his
helpless shoulders and
pull him here and there over the floor while he hung
his huge head

docilely over her shoulder and made futile dummy motions with his
feet. His hind legs danced in a manner all their own, chiefly by
hopping first on one foot and then on the other. Never being sure
whether dancing was going on or not, the hind legs played safe by
going through a series of steps whenever the music started playing. So
the spectacle was frequently presented of the front part of the camel
standing at ease and the rear keeping up a constant energetic motion
calculated to rouse a sympathetic perspiration in any soft-hearted
observer.

He was frequently favored. He danced first with a tall lady covered
with straw who announced jovially that she was a bale of hay and coyly
begged him not to eat her.

"I'd like to; you're so sweet," said the camel gallantly.

Each time the ringmaster shouted his call of "Men up!" he lumbered
ferociously for Betty with the cardboard wienerwurst or the photograph
of the bearded lady or whatever the favor chanced to be. Sometimes he
reached her first, but usually his rushes were unsuccessful and
resulted in intense interior arguments.

"For Heaven's sake," Perry would snarl, fiercely between his clenched
teeth, "get a little pep! I could have gotten her that time if you'd
picked your feet up."

"Well, gimme a little warnin'!"

"I did, darn you."

"I can't see a dog-gone thing in here."

"All you have to do is follow me. It's just like dragging a load of
sand round to walk with you."

"Maybe you wanta try back hare."

"You shut up! If these people found you in this room they'd give you
the worst beating you ever had. They'd take your taxi license away
from you!"

Perry surprised himself by the ease with which he made this monstrous
threat, but it seemed to have a soporific influence on his companion,
for he gave out an "aw gwan" and subsided into abashed silence.

The ringmaster mounted to the top of the piano and waved his hand for
silence.

"Prizes!" he cried. "Gather round!"

"Yea! Prizes!"

Self-consciously the circle swayed forward. The rather pretty girl who

had mustered the nerve to come as a bearded lady trembled with
excitement, thinking to be rewarded for an evening's hideousness. The
man who had spent the afternoon having tattoo marks painted on him
skulked on the edge of the crowd, blushing furiously when any one told
him he was sure to get it.

"Lady and gent performers of this circus," announced the ringmaster
jovially, "I am sure we will all agree that a good time has been had
by all. We will now bestow honor where honor is due by bestowing the
prizes. Mrs. Townsend has asked me to bestow the prices. Now, fellow
performers, the first prize is for that lady who has displayed this
evening the most striking, becoming"--at this point the bearded lady
sighed resignedly--"and original costume." Here the bale of hay
pricked up her ears. "Now I am sure that the decision which has been

agreed upon will be unanimous with all here present. The first prize
goes to Miss Betty Medill, the charming Egyptian snake-charmer." There
was a burst of applause, chiefly masculine, and Miss Betty Medill,
blushing beautifully through her olive paint, was passed up to receive
her award. With a tender glance the ringmaster handed down to her a
huge bouquet of orchids.

"And now," he continued, looking round him, "the other prize is for
that man who has the most amusing and original costume. This prize
goes without dispute to a guest in our midst, a gentleman who is
visiting here but whose stay we all hope will be long and merry--in
short, to the noble camel who has entertained us all by his hungry
look and his brilliant dancing throughout the evening."

He ceased and there was a violent clapping, and yeaing, for it was a
popular choice. The prize, a large box of cigars, was put aside for
the camel, as he was anatomically unable to accept it in person.

"And now," continued the ringmaster, "we will wind up the cotillion
with the marriage of Mirth to Folly!

"Form for the grand wedding march, the beautiful snake-charmer and the
noble camel in front!"

Betty skipped forward cheerily and wound an olive arm round the
camel's neck. Behind them formed the procession of little boys, little
girls, country jakes, fat ladies, thin men, sword-swallowers, wild men
of Borneo, and armless wonders, many of them well in their cups, all
of them excited and happy and dazzled by the flow of light and color

round them, and by the familiar faces, strangely unfamiliar under
bizarre wigs and barbaric paint. The voluptuous chords of the wedding
march done in blasphemous syncopation issued in a delirious blend from
the trombones and saxophones--and the march began.

"Aren't you glad, camel?" demanded Betty sweetly as they stepped off.
"Aren't you glad we're going to be married and you're going to belong
to the nice snake-charmer ever afterward?"

The camel's front legs pranced, expressing excessive joy.

"Minister! Minister! Where's the minister?" cried voices out of the
revel. "Who's going to be the clergyman?"

The head of Jumbo, obese negro, waiter at the Tally-ho Club for many
years, appeared rashly through a half-opened pantry door.

"Oh, Jumbo!"

"Get old Jumbo. He's the fella!"

"Come on, Jumbo. How 'bout marrying us a couple?"

"Yea!"

Jumbo was seized by four comedians, stripped of his apron, and
escorted to a raised daïs at the head of the ball. There his collar
was removed and replaced back side forward with ecclesiastical effect.
The parade separated into two lines, leaving an aisle for the bride
and groom.

"Lawdy, man," roared Jumbo, "Ah got ole Bible 'n' ev'ythin', sho
nuff."

He produced a battered Bible from an interior pocket.

"Yea! Jumbo's got a Bible!"

"Razor, too, I'll bet!"

Together the snake-charmer and the camel ascended
the cheering aisle
and stopped in front of Jumbo.

"Where's yo license, camel?"

A man near by prodded Perry.

"Give him a piece of paper. Anything'll do."

Perry fumbled confusedly in his pocket, found a
folded paper, and
pushed it out through the camel's mouth. Holding it
upside down Jumbo
pretended to scan it earnestly.

"Dis yeah's a special camel's license," he said. "Get
you ring ready,
camel."

Inside the camel Perry turned round and addressed
his worse half.

"Gimme a ring, for Heaven's sake!"

"I ain't got none," protested a weary voice.

"You have. I saw it."

"I ain't goin' to take it offen my hand."

"If you don't I'll kill you."

There was a gasp and Perry felt a huge affair of rhinestone and brass
inserted into his hand.

Again he was nudged from the outside.

"Speak up!"

"I do!" cried Perry quickly.

He heard Betty's responses given in a debonair tone, and even in this
burlesque the sound thrilled him.

Then he had pushed the rhinestone through a tear in the camel's coat and was slipping it on her finger, muttering ancient and historic

words after Jumbo. He didn't want any one to know about this ever. His

one idea was to slip away without having to disclose his identity, for

Mr. Tate had so far kept his secret well. A dignified young man,

Perry--and this might injure his infant law practice.

"Embrace the bride!"

"Unmask, camel, and kiss her!"

Instinctively his heart beat high as Betty turned to him laughingly

and began to strike the card-board muzzle. He felt his self-control

giving way, he longed to surround her with his arms and declare his

identity and kiss those lips that smiled only a foot away--when

suddenly the laughter and applause round them died off and a curious

hush fell over the hall. Perry and Betty looked up in surprise. Jumbo

had given vent to a huge "Hello!" in such a startled voice that all
eyes were bent on him.

"Hello!" he said again. He had turned round the camel's marriage
license, which he had been holding upside down, produced spectacles,
and was studying it agonizingly.

"Why," he exclaimed, and in the pervading silence his words were heard
plainly by every one in the room, "this yeah's a sho-nuff marriage
permit."

"What?"

"Huh?"

"Say it again, Jumbo!"

"Sure you can read?"

Jumbo waved them to silence and Perry's blood burned to fire in his veins as he realized the break he had made.

"Yassuh!" repeated Jumbo. "This yeah's a sho-nuff license, and the
pa'ties concerned one of 'em is dis yeah young lady, Miz Betty Medill,
and th' other's Mistah Perry Pa'khurst."

There was a general gasp, and a low rumble broke out as all eyes fell
on the camel. Betty shrank away from him quickly, her tawny eyes
giving out sparks of fury.

"Is you Mistah Pa'khurst, you camel?"

Perry made no answer. The crowd pressed up closer and stared at him.
He stood frozen rigid with embarrassment, his cardboard face still
hungry and sardonic as he regarded the ominous Jumbo.

"Y'all bettah speak up!" said Jumbo slowly, "this yeah's a mighty

203

serious mattah. Outside mah duties at this club ah happens to be a
sho-nuff minister in the Firs' Cullud Baptis' Church. It done look to
me as though y'all is gone an' got married."

V

The scene that followed will go down forever in the annals of the
Tallyho Club. Stout matrons fainted, one hundred per cent Americans
swore, wild-eyed débutantes babbled in lightning groups instantly
formed and instantly dissolved, and a great buzz of chatter, virulent
yet oddly subdued, hummed through the chaotic ballroom. Feverish
youths swore they would kill Perry or Jumbo or themselves or some one,
and the Baptis' preacheh was besieged by a tempestuous covey of
clamorous amateur lawyers, asking questions, making threats, demanding

precedents, ordering the bonds annulled, and especially trying to
ferret out any hint of prearrangement in what had occurred.

In the corner Mrs. Townsend was crying softly on the shoulder of Mr.
Howard Tate, who was trying vainly to comfort her; they were
exchanging "all my fault's" volubly and voluminously. Outside on a
snow-covered walk Mr. Cyrus Medill, the Aluminum Man, was being paced
slowly up and down between two brawny charioteers, giving vent now to
a string of unrepeatables, now to wild pleadings that they'd just let
him get at Jumbo. He was facetiously attired for the evening as a wild
man of Borneo, and the most exacting stage-manager would have
acknowledged any improvement in casting the part to be quite
impossible.

Meanwhile the two principals held the real centre of the stage. Betty
Medill--or was it Betty Parkhurst?--storming furiously, was surrounded
by the plainer girls--the prettier ones were too busy talking about
her to pay much attention to her--and over on the other side of the
hall stood the camel, still intact except for his headpiece, which
dangled pathetically on his chest. Perry was earnestly engaged in
making protestations of his innocence to a ring of angry, puzzled men.
Every few minutes, just as he had apparently proved his case, some one
would mention the marriage certificate, and the inquisition would
begin again.

A girl named Marion Cloud, considered the second best belle of Toledo,
changed the gist of the situation by a remark she made to Betty.

"Well," she said maliciously, "it'll all blow over, dear. The courts
will annul it without question."

Betty's angry tears dried miraculously in her eyes, her lips shut
tight together, and she looked stonily at Marion. Then she rose and,
scattering her sympathizers right and left, walked directly across the
room to Perry, who stared at her in terror. Again silence crept down
upon the room.

"Will you have the decency to grant me five minutes' conversation--or
wasn't that included in your plans?"

He nodded, his mouth unable to form words.

Indicating coldly that he was to follow her she walked out into the
hall with her chin uptilted and headed for the privacy of one of the
little card-rooms.

Perry started after her, but was brought to a jerky halt by the
failure of his hind legs to function.

"You stay here!" he commanded savagely.

"I can't," whined a voice from the hump, "unless you get out first and
let me get out."

Perry hesitated, but unable any longer to tolerate the eyes of the
curious crowd he muttered a command and the camel moved carefully from
the room on its four legs.

Betty was waiting for him.

"Well," she began furiously, "you see what you've done! You and that
crazy license! I told you you shouldn't have gotten it!"

"My dear girl, I--"

"Don't say 'dear girl' to me! Save that for your real wife if you ever
get one after this disgraceful performance. And don't try to pretend
it wasn't all arranged. You know you gave that colored waiter money!
You know you did! Do you mean to say you didn't try to marry me?"

"No--of course--"

"Yes, you'd better admit it! You tried it, and now what are you going
to do? Do you know my father's nearly crazy? It'll serve you right if
he tries to kill you. He'll take his gun and put some cold steel in
you. Even if this wed--this _thing_ can be annulled it'll hang
over me all the rest of my life!"

Perry could not resist quoting softly: "'Oh, camel, wouldn't you like
to belong to the pretty snake-charmer for all your--"

"Shut-up!" cried Betty.

There was a pause.

"Betty," said Perry finally, "there's only one thing to do that will
really get us out clear. That's for you to marry me."

"Marry you!"

"Yes. Really it's the only--"

"You shut up! I wouldn't marry you if--if--"

"I know. If I were the last man on earth. But if you care anything
about your reputation--"

"Reputation!" she cried. "You're a nice one to think about my
reputation _now_. Why didn't you think about my reputation before
you hired that horrible Jumbo to--to--"

Perry tossed up his hands hopelessly.

"Very well. I'll do anything you want. Lord knows I renounce all
claims!"

"But," said a new voice, "I don't."

Perry and Betty started, and she put her hand to her heart.

"For Heaven's sake, what was that?"

"It's me," said the camel's back.

In a minute Perry had whipped off the camel's skin, and a lax, limp
object, his clothes hanging on him damply, his hand clenched tightly
on an almost empty bottle, stood defiantly before them.

"Oh," cried Betty, "you brought that object in here to frighten me!
You told me he was deaf--that awful person!"

The camel's back sat down on a chair with a sigh of satisfaction.

"Don't talk 'at way about me, lady. I ain't no person. I'm your husband."

"Husband!"

The cry was wrung simultaneously from Betty and Perry.

"Why, sure. I'm as much your husband as that gink is. The smoke didn't marry you to the camel's front. He married you to the whole camel. Why, that's my ring you got on your finger!"

With a little yelp she snatched the ring from her finger and flung it passionately at the floor.

"What's all this?" demanded Perry dazedly.

"Jes' that you better fix me an' fix me right. If you don't I'm a-gonna have the same claim you got to bein' married to her!"

"That's bigamy," said Perry, turning gravely to Betty.

Then came the supreme moment of Perry's evening, the ultimate chance
on which he risked his fortunes. He rose and looked first at Betty,
where she sat weakly, aghast at this new complication, and then at the
individual who swayed from side to side on his chair, uncertainly,
menacingly.

"Very well," said Perry slowly to the individual, "you can have her.
Betty, I'm going to prove to you that as far as I'm concerned our
marriage was entirely accidental. I'm going to renounce utterly my
rights to have you as my wife, and give you to--to the man whose ring
you wear--your lawful husband."

There was a pause and four horror-stricken eyes were turned on him,

"Good-by, Betty," he said brokenly. "Don't forget me in your new-found
happiness. I'm going to leave for the Far West on the morning train.
Think of me kindly, Betty."

With a last glance at them he turned and his head rested on his chest
as his hand touched the door-knob.

"Good-by," he repeated. He turned the door-knob.

But at this sound the snakes and silk and tawny hair precipitated
themselves violently toward him.

"Oh, Perry, don't leave me! Perry, Perry, take me with you!"

Her tears flowed damply on his neck. Calmly he folded his arms about
her.

"I don't care," she cried. "I love you and if you can wake up a

minister at this hour and have it done over again I'll go West with
you."

Over her shoulder the front part of the camel looked at the back part
of the camel--and they exchanged a particularly subtle, esoteric sort
of wink that only true camels can understand.

fin

Fenimore Cooper's Literary Offences

Mark Twain

"The Pathfinder" and "The Deerslayer" stand at the head of Cooper's novels as artistic creations. There are others of his works which contain parts as perfect as are to be found in these, and scenes even more thrilling. Not one can be compared with either of them as a finished whole. The defects in both of these tales are comparatively slight. They were pure works of art.

--Professor Lounsbury

The five tales reveal an extraordinary fullness of invention. ... One of the very greatest characters in fiction, Natty Bumppo... The craft of the woodsman, the tricks of the trapper, all the delicate art of the forest were familiar to Cooper from his youth up.

--Professor Matthews

Cooper is the greatest artist in the domain of romantic fiction in America.

--Wilkie Collins

It seems to me that it was far from right for the Professor of English Literature at Yale, the Professor of English Literature in Columbia, and Wilkie Collins to deliver opinions on Cooper's literature without having read some of it. It would have been much more decorous to keep silent and let persons talk who have read Cooper.

Cooper's art has some defects. In one place in "Deerslayer," and in the restricted space of two-thirds of a page, Cooper has scored 114 offenses against literary art out of a possible 115. It breaks the record.

There are nineteen rules governing literary art in domain of romantic fiction -- some say twenty-two. In "Deerslayer," Cooper violated eighteen of them. These eighteen require:

1. That a tale shall accomplish something and arrive somewhere. But the "Deerslayer" tale accomplishes nothing and arrives in air.

2. They require that the episodes in a tale shall be necessary parts of the tale, and shall help to develop it. But as the "Deerslayer" tale is not a tale, and accomplishes nothing and arrives nowhere, the episodes have no rightful place in the work, since there was nothing for them to develop.

3. They require that the personages in a tale shall be alive, except in the case of corpses, and that always the reader shall be able to tell the corpses from the others. But this detail has often been overlooked in the "Deerslayer" tale.

4. They require that the personages in a tale, both dead and alive, shall exhibit a sufficient excuse for being there. But this detail also has been overlooked in the "Deerslayer" tale.

5. The require that when the personages of a tale deal in conversation, the talk shall sound like human talk, and be talk such as human beings would be likely to talk in the given circumstances, and have a discoverable meaning, also a discoverable purpose, and a show of relevancy, and remain in the neighborhood of the subject at hand, and be interesting to the reader, and help out the tale, and stop when the people cannot think of anything more to say. But this requirement has been ignored from the beginning of the "Deerslayer" tale to the end of it.

6. They require that when the author describes the character of a personage in the tale, the conduct and conversation of that personage shall justify said description. But this law gets little or no attention in the "Deerslayer" tale, as Natty Bumppo's case will amply prove.

7. They require that when a personage talks like an illustrated, gilt-edged, tree-calf, hand-tooled, seven-dollar Friendship's Offering in the beginning of a paragraph, he shall not talk like a negro minstrel in the end of it. But this rule is flung down and danced upon in the "Deerslayer" tale.

8. They require that crass stupidities shall not be played upon the reader as "the craft of the woodsman, the delicate art of the forest," by either the author or the people in the tale. But this rule is persistently violated in the "Deerslayer" tale.

9. They require that the personages of a tale shall confine themselves to possibilities and let miracles alone; or, if they venture a miracle, the author must so plausibly set it forth as to make it look possible and reasonable. But these rules are not respected in the "Deerslayer" tale.

10. They require that the author shall make the reader feel a deep interest in the personages of his tale and in their fate; and that he shall make the reader love the good people in the tale and hate the bad ones. But the reader of the "Deerslayer" tale dislikes the good people in it, is indifferent to the others, and wishes they would all get drowned together.

11. They require that the characters in a tale shall be so clearly defined that the reader can tell beforehand

what each will do in a given emergency. But in the "Deerslayer" tale, this rule is vacated.

In addition to these large rules, there are some little ones. These require that the author shall:

12. *Say* what he is proposing to say, not merely come near it.

13. Use the right word, not its second cousin.

14. Eschew surplusage.

15. Not omit necessary details.

16. Avoid slovenliness of form.

17. Use good grammar.

18. Employ a simple and straightforward style.

Even these seven are coldly and persistently violated in the "Deerslayer" tale.

Cooper's gift in the way of invention was not a rich endowment; but such as it was he liked to work it, he was pleased with the effects, and indeed he did some quite sweet things with it. In his little box of stage-properties he kept six or eight cunning devices, tricks, artifices for his savages and woodsmen to deceive and circumvent each other with, and he was never so happy as when he was working these innocent things and seeing them go. A favorite one was to make a moccasined person tread in the tracks of a moccasined enemy, and thus hide his own trail. Cooper wore out barrels and barrels of moccasins in working that trick. Another stage-property that he pulled out of his box pretty frequently was the broken twig. He prized his broken twig above all the rest of his effects, and worked it the hardest. It is a restful chapter in any book of his when somebody doesn't step on a dry twig and alarm all the reds and whites for two hundred yards around. Every time a Cooper person is in peril, and absolute silence is worth four dollars a minute, he is sure to step on a dry twig. There may be a hundred other handier things to step on, but that wouldn't satisfy Cooper. Cooper requires him to turn out and find a dry twig; and if he can't do it, go and borrow one. In fact, the Leatherstocking Series ought to have been called the Broken Twig Series.

I am sorry that there is not room to put in a few dozen instances of the delicate art of the forest, as practiced by Natty Bumppo and some of the other Cooperian experts. Perhaps we may venture two or three samples. Cooper was a sailor -- a naval officer; yet he gravely tells us how a vessel, driving toward a lee shore in a gale, is steered for a particular spot by her skipper because he knows of an *undertow* there which will hold her back against the gale and save her. For just pure woodcraft, or sailorcraft, or whatever it is, isn't that neat? For several years, Cooper was daily in the society of artillery, and he ought to have noticed that when a cannon-ball strikes the ground it either buries itself or skips a hundred feet or so; skips again a hundred feet or so -- and so on, till finally it gets tired and rolls. Now in one place he loses some "females" -- as he always calls women -- in the edge of a wood near a plain at night in a fog, on purpose to give Bumppo a chance to show off the delicate art of the forest before the reader. These mislaid people are hunting for a fort. They hear a cannon-blast, and a cannon-ball presently comes rolling into the wood and stops at their feet. To the females this suggests nothing. The case is very different with the admirable Bumppo. I wish I may never know peace again if he doesn't strike out promptly and *follow the track* of that cannon-ball across the plain in the dense fog and find the fort. Isn't it a daisy? If Cooper had any real knowledge of Nature's ways of doing things, he had a most delicate art in concealing the fact. For instance: one of his acute Indian experts, Chingachgook (pronounced Chicago, I think), has lost the trail of a person he is tracking through the forest. Apparently that trail is hopelessly lost. Neither you nor I could ever have guessed the way to find it. It was very different with Chicago. Chicago was not stumped for long. He turned a running stream out of its course, and there, in the slush in its old bed, were that person's moccasin tracks. The current did not wash them away, as it would have done in all other like cases -- no, even the eternal laws of Nature have to vacate when Cooper wants to put up a delicate job of woodcraft on the reader.

We must be a little wary when Brander Matthews tells us that Cooper's books "reveal an extraordinary fullness of invention." As a rule, I am quite willing to accept Brander Matthews's literary judgments and applaud his lucid and graceful phrasing of them; but that particular statement needs to be taken with a few tons of salt. Bless you heart, Cooper hadn't any more invention than a horse; and don't mean a high-class horse, either; I mean a clothes- horse. It would be very difficult to find a really clever "situation" in Cooper's books, and still more difficult to find one of any kind which has failed to render absurd by his handling of it. Look at the episodes of "the caves"; and at the celebrated scuffle between Maqua and those others on the table-land a few days later; and at Hurry Harry's queer water-transit from the castle to the ark; and at Deerslayer's half-hour with his first corpse; and at the quarrel between Hurry Harry and Deerslayer later; and at -- but choose for yourself; you can't go amiss.

If Cooper had been an observer his inventive faculty would have worked better; not more interestingly, but more rationally, more plausibly. Cooper's proudest creations in the way of "situations" suffer noticeably from the absence of the observer's protecting gift. Cooper's eye was splendidly inaccurate. Cooper seldom saw anything correctly. He saw nearly all things as through a glass eye, darkly. Of course a man who cannot see the commonest little every-day matters accurately is working at a disadvantage when he is constructing a "situation." In the "Deerslayer" tale Cooper has a stream which is fifty feet wide where it flows out of a lake; it presently narrows to twenty as it meanders along for no given reason, and yet when a stream acts like that it ought to be required to explain itself. Fourteen pages later the width of the brook's outlet from the lake has suddenly shrunk thirty feet, and become "the narrowest part of the stream." This shrinkage is not accounted for. The stream has bends in it, a sure indication that it has alluvial banks and cuts them; yet these bends are only thirty and fifty feet long. If Cooper had been a nice and punctilious observer he would have noticed that the bends were often nine hundred feet long than short of it.

Cooper made the exit of that stream fifty feet wide, in the first place, for no particular reason; in the second place, he narrowed it to less than twenty to accommodate some Indians. He bends a "sapling" to form an arch over this narrow passage, and conceals six Indians in its foliage. They are "laying" for a settler's scow or ark which is coming up the stream on its way to the lake; it is being hauled against the stiff current by rope whose stationary end is anchored in the lake; its rate of progress cannot be more than a mile an hour. Cooper describes the ark, but pretty obscurely. In the matter of dimensions "it was little more than a modern canal boat." Let us guess, then, that it was about one hundred and forty feet long. It was of "greater breadth than common." Let us guess then that it was about sixteen feet wide. This leviathan had been prowling down bends which were but a third as long as itself, and scraping between banks where it only had two feet of space to spare on each side. We cannot too much admire this miracle. A low- roofed dwelling occupies "two-thirds of the ark's length" -- a dwelling ninety feet long and sixteen feet wide, let us say -- a kind of vestibule train. The dwelling has two rooms -- each forty- five feet long and sixteen feet wide, let us guess. One of them is the bedroom of the Hutter girls, Judith and Hetty; the other is the parlor in the daytime, at night it is papa's bedchamber. The ark is arriving at the stream's exit now, whose width has been reduced to less than twenty feet to accommodate the Indians -- say to eighteen. There is a foot to spare on each side of the boat. Did the Indians notice that there was going to be a tight squeeze there? Did they notice that they could make money by climbing down out of that arched sapling and just stepping aboard when the ark scraped by? No, other Indians would have noticed these things, but Cooper's Indian's never notice anything. Cooper thinks they are marvelous creatures for noticing, but he was almost always in error about his Indians. There was seldom a sane one among them.

The ark is one hundred and forty-feet long; the dwelling is ninety feet long. The idea of the Indians is to drop softly and secretly from the arched sapling to the dwelling as the ark creeps along under it at the rate of a mile an hour, and butcher the family. It will take the ark a minute and a half to pass under. It will take the ninety-foot dwelling a minute to pass under. Now, then, what did the six Indians do? It would take you thirty years to guess, and even then you would have to give it up, I believe. Therefore, I will tell you what the Indians did. Their chief, a person of quite extraordinary intellect for a Cooper Indian, warily watched the canal-boat as it squeezed along under him and when he had got his calculations fined down to exactly the right shade, as he judge, he let go and dropped. And *missed the boat*! That is actually what he did. He missed the house, and landed in he stern of the scow. It was not much of a fall, yet it knocked him silly. He lay there unconscious. If the house had been ninety-seven feet long he would have made the trip. The error lay in the construction of the house. Cooper was no architect.

There still remained in the roost five Indians. The boat has passed under and is now out of their reach. Let me explain what the five did -- you would not be able to reason it out for yourself. No. 1 jumped for the boat, but fell in the water astern of it. Then No. 2 jumped for the boat, but fell in the water still further astern of it. Then No. 3 jumped for the boat, and fell a good way astern of it. Then No. 4 jumped for the boat, and fell in the water *away* astern. Then even No. 5 made a jump for the boat -- for he was Cooper Indian. In that matter of intellect, the difference between a Cooper Indian and the Indian that stands in front of the cigar-shop is not spacious. The scow episode is really a sublime burst of invention; but it does not thrill, because the inaccuracy of details throw a sort of air of fictitiousness and general improbability over it. This comes of Cooper's inadequacy as observer.

The reader will find some examples of Cooper's high talent for inaccurate observation in the account of the shooting-match in "The Pathfinder."

A common wrought nail was driven lightly into the target, its head having been first touched with paint.

The color of the paint is not stated -- an important omission, but Cooper deals freely in important omissions. No, after all, it was not an important omission; for this nail-head is *a hundred yards from* the marksmen, and could not be seen at that distance, no matter what its color might be. How far can the best eyes see a common housefly? A hundred yards? It is quite impossible. Very well; eyes that cannot see a house-fly that is a hundred yards away cannot see an ordinary nail-head at that distance, for the size of the two objects is the same. It takes a keen eye to see a fly or a nail-head at fifty yards -- one hundred and fifty-feet. Can the reader do it?

The nail was lightly driven, its head painted, and game called. Then the Cooper miracles began. The bullet of the first marksman chipped an edge of the nail-head; the next man's bullet drove the nail a little way into the target -- and removed all the paint. Haven't the miracles gone far enough now? Not to suit Cooper; for the purpose of this whole scheme is to show off his prodigy, Deerslayer-Hawkeye-Long-Rifle-Leatherstocking-Pathfinder-Bumppo before the ladies.

"Be all ready to clench it, boys!" cried out Pathfinder, stepping into his friend's tracks the instant they were vacant. "Never mind a new nail; I can see that, though the paint is gone, and what I can see I can hit at a hundred yards, though it were only a mosquito's eye. Be ready to clench!" The rifle cracked, the bullet sped its way, and the

head of the nail was buried in the wood, covered by the piece of flattened lead.

There, you see, is a man who could hunt flies with a rifle, and command a ducal salary in a Wild West show to-day if we had him back with us.

The recorded feat is certainly surprising just as it stands; but it is not surprising enough for Cooper. Cooper adds a touch. He has made Pathfinder do this miracle with another man's rife; and not only that, but Pathfinder did not have even the advantage of loading it himself. He had everything against him, and yet he made that impossible shot; and not only made it, but did it with absolute confidence, saying, "Be ready to clench." Now a person like that would have undertaken that same feat with a brickbat, and with Cooper to help he would have achieved it, too.

Pathfinder showed off handsomely that day before the ladies. His very first feat a thing which no Wild West show can touch. He was standing with the group of marksmen, observing -- a hundred yards from the target, mind; one Jasper rasper raised his rifle and drove the center of the bull's-eye. Then the Quartermaster fired. The target exhibited no result this time. There was a laugh. "It's a dead miss," said Major Lundie. Pathfinder waited an impressive moment or two; then said, in that calm, indifferent, know-it-all way of his, "No, Major, he has covered

Jasper's bullet, as will be seen if any one will take the trouble to examine the target."

Wasn't it remarkable! How *could* he see that little pellet fly through the air and enter that distant bullet-hole? Yet that is what he did; for nothing is impossible to a Cooper person. Did any of those people have any deep-seated doubts about this thing? No; for that would imply sanity, and these were all Cooper people.

The respect for Pathfinder's skill and for his *quickness and accuracy of sight* [the italics are mine] was so profound and general, that the instant he made this declaration the spectators began to distrust their own opinions, and a dozen rushed to the target in order to ascertain the fact. There, sure enough, it was found that the Quartermaster's bullet had gone through the hole made by Jasper's, and that, too, so accurately as to require a minute examination to be certain of the circumstance, which, however, was soon clearly established by discovering one bullet over the other in the stump against which the target was placed.

They made a "minute" examination; but never mind, how could they know that there were two bullets in that hole without digging the latest one out? for neither probe nor eyesight could prove the presence of any more than one bullet. Did they dig? No; as we shall see. It is the Pathfinder's turn now; he steps out before the ladies, takes aim, and fires.

But, alas! here is a disappointment; in incredible, an unimaginable disappointment -- for the target's aspect is unchanged; there is nothing there but that same old bullet hole!

îIf one dared to hint at such a thing," cried Major Duncan, "I should say that the Pathfinder has also missed the target."

As nobody had missed it yet, the "also" was not necessary; but never mind about that, for the Pathfinder is going to speak.

"No, no, Major," said he, confidently, "that *would* be a risky declaration. I didn't load the piece, and can't say what was in it; but if it was lead, you will find the bullet driving down those of the Quartermaster and Jasper, else is not my name Pathfinder."

A shout from the target announced the truth of this assertion.

Is the miracle sufficient as it stands? Not for Cooper. The Pathfinder speaks again, as he "now slowly advances toward the stage occupied by the females":

"That's not all, boys, that's not all; if you find the target touched at all, I'll own to a miss. The

Quartermaster cut the wood, but you'll find no wood cut by that last messenger."

The miracle is at last complete. He knew -- doubtless *saw* -- at the distance of a hundred yards -- this his bullet had passed into the hole *without fraying the edges.* There were now three bullets in that one hole -- three bullets embedded processionally in the body of the stump back of the target. Everybody knew this -- somehow or other -- and yet nobody had dug any of them out to make sure. Cooper is not a close observer, but he is interesting. He is certainly always that, no matter what happens. And he is more interesting when he is not noticing what he is about than when he is. This is a considerable merit.

The conversations in the Cooper books have a curious sound in our modern ears. To believe that such talk really ever came out of people's mouths would be to believe that there was a time when time was of no value to a person who thought he had something to say; when it was the custom to spread a two-minute remark out to ten; when a man's mouth was a rolling-mill, and busied itself all day long in turning four-foot pigs of thought into thirty-foot bars of conversational railroad iron by attenuation; when subjects were seldom faithfully stuck to, but the talk wandered all around and arrived nowhere; when conversations consisted mainly of irrelevancies, with here and there a relevancy, a relevancy with an embarrassed look, as not being able to explain how it got there.

Cooper was certainly not a master in the construction of dialogue. Inaccurate observation defeated him here as it defeated him in so many other enterprises of his life. He even failed to notice that the man who talks corrupt English six days in the week must and will talk it on seventh, and can't help himself. In the "Deerslayer" story, he lets Deerslayer talk the showiest kind of book-talk sometimes, and at other times the basest of base dialects. For instance, when some one asks him if he has a sweetheart, and if so, where she abides, this is his majestic answer:

îShe's in the forest -- hanging from the boughs of the trees, in a soft rain -- in the dew on the open grass -- the clouds that float about in the blue heavens -- the birds that sing in the woods -- the sweet springs where I slake my thirst -- and in all the other glorious gifts that come from God's Providence!"

And he preceded that, a little before, with this:
"It consarns me as all things that touches a friend consarns a friend."

And this is another of his remarks:
"If I was Injin born, now, I might tell of this, or carry in the scalp and boast of the expl'ite afore

the whole tribe; of if my inimy had only been a bear" -- [and so on]

We cannot imagine such a thing as a veteran Scotch Commander-in- Chief comporting himself like a windy melodramatic actor, but Cooper could. On one occasion, Alice and Cora were being chased by the French through a fog in the neighborhood of their father's fort:

îPoint de quartier aux coquins!î **cried an eager pursuer, who seemed to direct the operations of the enemy.**

"Stand firm and be ready, my gallant 60ths!" suddenly exclaimed a voice above them; "wait to see the enemy, fire low, and sweep the glacis."

"Father! father" exclaimed a piercing cry from out the mist. "It is I! Alice! thy own Elsie! spare, O! save your daughters!"
"Hold!" shouted the former speaker, in the awful tones of parental agony, the sound reaching even to the woods, and rolling back in a solemn echo. "'Tis she! God has restored me my children! Throw open the sally- port; to the field, 60ths, to the field! pull not a trigger, lest ye kill my lambs! Drive off these dogs of France with your steel!"

Cooper's word-sense was singularly dull. When a person has a poor ear for music he will flat and sharp right along without knowing it. He keeps near the tune, but is *not* the tune. When a person has a poor ear for words, the result is a literary flatting and sharping; you perceive what he is intending to say, but you also perceive that he does not *say* it. This is Cooper. He was not a word-musician. His ear was satisfied with the *approximate* words. I will furnish some circumstantial evidence in support of this charge. My instances are gathered from half a dozen pages of the tale called "Deerslayer." He uses "Verbal" for "oral"; "precision" for "facility"; "phenomena" for "marvels"; "necessary" for "predetermined"; "unsophisticated" for "primitive"; "preparation" for "expectancy"; "rebuked" for "subdued"; "dependent on" for "resulting from"; "fact" for "condition"; "fact" for "conjecture"; "precaution" for "caution"; "explain" for "determine"; "mortified" for "disappointed"; "meretricious" for "factitious"; "materially" for "considerably"; "decreasing" for "deepening"; "increasing" for "disappearing"; "embedded" for "inclosed"; "treacherous" for "hostile"; "stood" for "stooped"; "softened" for "replaced"; "rejoined" for "remarked"; "situation" for "condition"; "different" for "differing"; "insensible" for "unsentient"; "brevity" for "celerity"; "distrusted" for "suspicious"; "mental imbecility" for "imbecility"; "eyes" for "sight"; "counteracting" for "opposing"; "funeral obsequies" for "obsequies."

There have been daring people in the world who claimed that Cooper could write English, but they are all dead now -- all dead but Lounsbury. I don't remember that Lounsbury makes the claim in so many words, still he makes it, for he says that "Deerslayer" is a "pure work of art." Pure, in that connection, means faultless -- faultless in all details -- and language is a detail. If Mr. Lounsbury had only compared Cooper's English with the English he writes himself -- but it is plain that he didn't; and so it is likely that he imagines until this day that Cooper's is as clean and compact as his own. Now I feel sure, deep down in my heart, that Cooper wrote about the poorest English that exists in our language, and that the English of "Deerslayer" is the very worst that even Cooper ever wrote.

I may be mistaken, but it does seem to me that "Deerslayer" is not a work of art in any sense; it does seem to me that it is destitute of every detail that goes to the making of a work of art; in truth, it seems to me that "Deerslayer" is just simply a literary *delirium tremens*.

A work of art? It has no invention; it has no order, system, sequence, or result; it has no lifelikeness, no thrill, no stir, no seeming of reality; its characters are confusedly drawn, and by their acts and words they prove that they are not the sort of people the author claims that they are; its humor is pathetic; its pathos is funny; its conversations are -- oh! indescribable; its love-scenes odious; its English a crime against the language.

Counting these out, what is left is Art. I think we must all admit that.

fin!

That's that!